"Double Canister At Ten Yards"

The Federal Artillery And The Repulse Of Pickett's Charge

By David Shultz

Copyright 1995

Rank And File Publications
1926 South Pacific Coast Highway Suite 228
Redondo Beach, California 90277

ISBN Number: 0-9638993-5-X
Library of Congress Number: 95-068439

Foreword

The role played by Union artillery at the Battle of Gettysburg has been long neglected. In many other Civil War battles, Union guns were unable to function effectively because so much of the fighting took place in heavily wooded terrain. This was not the case at Gettysburg, where the high ground and open fields made it an artillerist's dream.

Earlier Gettysburg historians, such as Bruce Catton, Edwin Coddington, George Stewart and Glenn Tucker, have ignored or downplayed the significance of the Union artillery in the repulse of Pickett's Charge.

Under the overall command of Brigadier General Henry J. Hunt, the guns of Colonel Charles Wainwright's and Major Thomas Osborn's batteries on the Union right as well as Lieutenant Colonel Freeman McGilvery's on the Union left, have never received the full credit due them for their work on July 3rd, 1863. One wonders what the outcome might have been without the excellent work of the men who manned these guns.

David Shultz has conducted exhaustive research to fill this gap. Although this study is in detail, it is only an overview, with much more to come. He is now preparing a more comprehensive book for future publication on the Union artillery during the entire Battle of Gettysburg.

This booklet is a must for all artillery buffs and serious students of the Battle of Gettysburg.

Charles Hathaway
Licensed Battlefield Guide
Gettysburg, Pennsylvania

"See 'em! See 'em!" shouted Brigadier General Henry J. Hunt as he emptied his revolver into the mass of gray and butternut-clad soldiers storming over the stone wall. It was nearing 3:45 p.m. on Friday, July 3rd, 1863. The Army of the Potomac, commanded by Major General George G. Meade, and the Army of Northern Virginia, commanded by General Robert E. Lee, were in the climax of a three-day death struggle. The Confederate assault against the Federal line on Cemetery Ridge would last less than one hour, but it would signal a turning point in America's bloody Civil War.

Henry Jackson Hunt, the 44-year-old Chief of Artillery for the Army of the Potomac, stood in his stirrups as he discharged his weapon. He had just ridden up through all the confusion to the position of Captain Andrew Cowan's 1st New York Independent Battery just south of the small grove we now call the Copse of Trees.[1] Cowan had five 3" Ordnance Rifles posted to the left of the trees, and his remaining gun was posted to their right. As Cowan's gunners discharged their last load of double canister, Hunt's horse, Bill, was shot. As Bill fell, Hunt had no time to clear the saddle. Both rider and horse hit the ground, pinning Hunt by one leg.

As Cowan began to prolonge (drag by hand using ropes) his five rifles to the rear, Rebels swarmed over the stone wall, passing Hunt and paying him no mind: Perhaps Cowan's battery seemed the better prize. As Hunt struggled to free himself, two of Cowan's cannoneers ran forward to help. After they jerked Hunt to his feet, they disappeared back over the ridge. Hunt stood dazed, but unhurt. He noticed that Cowan's battery, partially concealed by its own smoke, was disappearing back over the ridge as Yankee reinforcements converged on the thickets.

As far north as the eye could see, Confederate battle flags were now soaring over the wall. Confederate artillery, pushed out to the Emmitsburg Road in support of the Charge, indiscriminately killed both friend and foe alike as Rebel shells exploded in the midst of the mob of men surrounding Hunt. Federal artillery posted east of the Copse of Trees fired their pieces over the top of their own line, causing many Union casualties as well.

Seeing no general officer about, Hunt unsuccessfully

attempted to take control of the chaos around him. He watched as one Federal infantryman was blown a dozen feet into the air and cart-wheeled ten feet back. For a moment, Hunt seemed bewildered by the confusion and ferocity around him. Soon the wild screaming and incessant musketry began to die down. He heard cheering to the north; the sound moved south down the line, toward the Copse of Trees. The Rebels were giving ground. It seemed to Hunt that the blue line, on impulse and without orders, all at once rushed forward. The few Rebels east of the wall that were not prisoners were either dead or wounded. The surviving Confederates retreated back across the Emmitsburg Road. The Union defense of Cemetery Ridge had succeeded; the Confederate charge had failed.

Hunt Sets Up His Line

About 4:30 a.m. on July 3rd, Hunt slowly arose from a three-hour nap as his chief of staff, Lieutenant Colonel E. R. Warner, handed him a cup of hot black coffee. Hunt was a career artilleryman. Born in 1819 on a U.S. Army post in Michigan into a family whose history already spanned two centuries of military service, he had decided at an early age that he, too, would choose the army as a career. Hunt graduated from West Point in 1839, ranking 19th out of 31 in his class. When the war broke out he was breveted major and from there quickly rose up the ranks. Between Bull Run and Chancellorsville he became well-known throughout the army for his coolness under fire, and at Malvern Hill in 1862 his handling of the artillery contributed materially to victory. Thoroughly professional, he was quick to criticize those who seemed to lack his commitment and effectiveness, and especially politically appointed officers.

As Hunt thanked Warner for the refreshing breakfast, a loud report showed that Federal artillery along the Baltimore Pike had opened the day's battle by firing on the enemy around the base of Culp's Hill. Hunt had spent most of the night working on placing and rebuilding batteries that had been wrecked in the fight on July 2nd. Hunt stated:

> The night of July 2nd was spent devoted in
> great part to repairing damages, replenishing
> ammunition chests, and reducing and
> reorganizing such batteries as had lost so many
> men, equipment and horses, as to be unable

efficiently to work the full number of guns assigned . . . By daylight the next morning this duty had been performed as good as possible, and, when it was found impossible to reorganize, the batteries were withdrawn and replaced by others from the Artillery Reserve. The work was completed by daylight of the 3rd.[2]

Hunt knew on the evening of July 2nd that the battle had not ended. Like most of the other general officers in the Army of the Potomac, he believed that another day of battle was just beginning, and he had a good deal of work yet to do. For the next several hours Hunt organized and prepared his defensive line. By one o'clock he had 175 guns in line covering the entire Federal position, including 132 between Little Round Top and Cemetery Hill. He had 95 more waiting just behind the middle of the lines, readily available for immediate action.

Hunt organized his weapons in good Napoleonic fashion into three distinct groups that could concentrate their fire to hit any enemy force that might approach the Cemetery Ridge line. Any attack would be subject to either "defilade" (direct) or "enfilade" (flank or side) fire. An attack on the center of the line, expected and predicted the previous evening by the commander of the army, Major General George Gordon Meade, would be the focus of a storm of shot and shell from all sides. The three groups were:

* *The south Cemetery Ridge line* (referred to normally as "McGilvery's line") extended from where the Pennsylvania monument now stands some 600 to 700 yards south. Controlled by Lieutenant Colonel Freeman McGilvery, commander of the 1st Volunteer Brigade, Reserve Artillery, this line commanded the Plum Run valley. Lieutenant Benjamin Rittenhouse's battery on Little Round Top gave it additional strength.

* *The Angle, or Cemetery Ridge line*, extended from Ziegler's Grove to the area south of the Copse of Trees. Nominally under the control of Captain John Hazard, commander of the II Corps artillery, this area was closely watched by Hunt and Major General Winfield Scott Hancock during the Charge. It commanded the field directly west of the stone wall, from south of the Codori farm to the Bliss farm.

* *Cemetery Hill* (also referred to as "Osborn's line"):

Under joint command of Colonel Charles Wainwright, commander of the I Corps artillery, and Major Thomas Osborn, commander of the XI Corps artillery, this line stretched across the top of the most dominant feature on the landscape, Cemetery Hill, and commanded the field from the McMillan house on the north end of Seminary Ridge to the Codori house. Nearly all of the area to be marched across by the men of Pettigrew and Trimble came under its direct fire.

* In addition, roughly one-half mile behind Cemetery Ridge sat the artillery park of the Army of the Potomac, perfectly located to reinforce any of the three groups. Here also waited the ammunition wagons, easily available in any emergency.

Hunt himself summarized his ideas about what was in store and how the artillery needed to be utilized on this day:

> It was of the first importance to have our line in the best possible condition to meet *the assault*, to which the cannonade would be a mere subordinate preliminary; and with that view to subject his troops from the first moment of their advance and whilst beyond musketry range to a heavy concentrated cross fire of artillery in order to break their formation, check their impulse and bring them in as disordered a condition and with as much loss as possible to the point of attack, and my orders were given specially with this view.[3]

Hunt carefully prepared his batteries and their commanders, instructing them on what to expect on this day and how to use their weapons in the most effective manner possible. By the time the Confederate attack was launched, Hunt had worked for some 10 hours, creating a powerful defensive line, one that would be extremely difficult for the enemy infantry to even reach, let alone break. That afternoon, he successfully and efficiently brought the full power of the artillery branch of the Army of the Potomac to bear against the Confederate assault, and did much to defeat it.

* * *

The early morning barrage in support of the XII Corps

on Culp's Hill lasted about fifteen minutes, then scaled down to sporadic fire for the rest of the morning. Hunt and Warner left the artillery park and rode over to the Baltimore Pike to see if everything was in order. The action in this area overshadowed a smaller barrage of artillery fire which took place along South Cemetery Ridge.

About the same time, 4:30 a.m., a Confederate artillery officer walked into the Sherfy Peach Orchard and looked with alarm at his exposed batteries. To the east, he could see the silhouetted form of a line of Federal guns 1,200 yards away. With dawn beginning to break and Federal infantry beginning to stir, he decided to pull his guns back before the Federals spied him.

The Federal guns that the Confederate had seen were probably the two 12-pounder Napoleons of Battery K of the 4th U. S. Artillery, commanded by Lieutenant Robert James, or the four Napoleons belonging to Lieutenant Edwin Dow's 6th Maine Light, posted to the right of Battery K.. They had been put into position at the end of hostilities on July 2nd. Their position was just north of the George Weikert house, covering the Trostle farm 700 yards to the west. They were about 100 yards behind an impromptu artillery line built by McGilvery. This new line would be reestablished and strengthened with additional batteries stretching north along Cemetery Ridge.

James had been relieved. As his men were beginning to move, the Confederate opened on him in order to cover his own withdrawal. James and Dow replied with spherical case, firing toward flashes from enemy guns along the Emmitsburg Road. Lucky was the word used to describe James' aim. The Confederate artilleryman later recalled that the first Federal round wounded some of the men of the Washington Artillery.[4] The Confederate guns were pulled back west of the road into a swale, ending the little duel. James pulled his two guns out and left for the rear, never knowing the results of his accurate fire. Battery K was finished at Gettysburg.[5]

Throughout the early morning hours of July 3rd, McGilvery had only 12 cannons on his line. James' two and four from Dow covering the Trostle farm lane, while six from Lieutenant Evan Thomas' 4th U. S. Battery C, a full 600 yards north of Dow, well below the crest of Cemetery Ridge, covered Plum Run. All three batteries were equipped with 12-pounder Napoleons.

As James pulled out, Captain Nelson Ames, 1st New

York Light, Battery G, pulled in with his six 12-pounder Napoleons. Ames attempted to dig in on an open shelf that sloped gently west toward a dry ravine. To his right Dow pulled out of line, heading back to the artillery park to refit.

For a few moments before sunrise on July 3rd, McGilvery's 700-yard line was covered by only Ames' and Thomas' guns, with the center completely exposed. The broken remnants of the III Corps, as well as the survivors of the 1st Division of the II Corps, held the ground between Ames and Thomas, but, for the most part, the line was left unreinforced. To fill the gap, McGilvery asked for, and received, artillery units that had been refitted during the night. Most of these units belonged to his own 1st Volunteer Brigade and were already veterans that had battled in the Peach Orchard the previous day.[6]

The first to arrive was Captain James Thompson's Pennsylvania Light, Consolidated Batteries C and F, with his five 3" Ordnance Rifles and 76 men. These combined batteries were just a shadow of their original strength. Thompson pulled into position on the left of Thomas, leaving a large gap of 70 yards in between. Following Thompson came Captain Patrick Hart, commanding the 15th New York Light Battery with four 12-pounder Napoleons. Not seeing McGilvery on the line, Hart reported to Thompson, who invited him to take up position on the left flank of his Pennsylvanians, which Hart did, leaving an open space of about 60 yards.[7] Pulling into position to the immediate right of Ames were four Napoleons from two different

10 Pounder Parrott Rifle (All photos courtesy Charles Hathaway)

batteries. The first section, commanded by Lieutenant Richard Milton of the 9th Massachusetts (Bigelow's) Light Battery, was followed by Lieutenant John G. Turnbull's section of the 3rd U. S. Artillery, consolidated Batteries F and K. Both batteries had been so badly chewed up on July 2nd that in order to be effective they had to be temporarily consolidated.[8] The two young lieutenants kept their commands separate but worked as one, though Milton was senior in rank and assumed responsibility of command. Turnbull, a U. S. regular veteran with four battles under his belt, accepted this situation and helped Milton, a rookie, reassemble his butchered command.

The last Peach Orchard veteran to pull into line was Captain Charles Phillips, commanding the 5th Massachusetts Light, Battery E (10th N.Y. attached.) Phillips pulled his six 3" Ordnance Rifles into the small space between Hart's right flank and Thompson's left. His six rifles were crammed only ten feet apart between the hubs. Because of casualties suffered on the previous day, all seven of these batteries were reinforced by infantrymen detached from their regiments.[9]

One other veteran unit of July 2nd was posted off Milton's right flank. Lieutenant William Rank's two Ordnance Rifles from the 3rd Pennsylvania Heavy Artillery, Battery H, had engaged the Stonewall Brigade along Brinkerhoff's Ridge on July 2nd in support of Colonel John McIntosh's cavalry brigade. It was the section's first engagement, and they had preformed brilliantly. Ready for more action, the Pennsylvania volunteers unlimbered on south Cemetery Ridge to the right front of Milton, leaving a huge gap of 100 yards. Filling most of this gap was the only battery that had not seen action on July 2nd, the Connecticut Light Artillery, 2nd Battery, commanded by Captain John W. Sterling, who had 106 men serving four 14-pounder James' rifles and two large-bored 12-pounder Howitzers. Welcomed by McGilvery, Sterling sat to Milton's immediate right, with his guns extending almost to Rank's section.

By about 6:30 a.m., McGilvery had created a strong line of artillery positions that would play a major part in the day's action. Meanwhile, Hunt and Warner visited the batteries to the east along Major General Henry W. Slocum's XII Corps line, observing the action along the Baltimore Pike.

Satisfied with what they saw, they decided to check on Osborn's and Wainwright's lines on Cemetery Hill. Col. Charles Wainwright, I Corps Artillery Brigade commander, was in charge of five batteries east of the Baltimore Pike outside the

"Prepare to Fire"

Evergreen Cemetery. Beginning on Wainwright's far right on Stevens' knoll and following Cemetery Hill north around to the northwest and west, the batteries were in the following order: Stevens' 5th Maine Light with six 12-pounders, commanded by Lieutenant Edward Whittier; Reynolds' 1st New York Battery L, with four 3" Ordnance Rifles, Lieutenant George Breck commanding, four 3" Ordnance Rifles from Captain Michael Weidrich's 1st New York Battery I; four 12-pounder Napoleons from Captain James Stewart's 4th U.S., Battery A, and Captain Bruce Ricketts' consolidated Pennsylvania Batteries F and G with six Ordnance Rifles.

Major Thomas Osborn, commander of the XI Corps Artillery Brigade, controlled seven batteries located west of the Pike in the Cemetery itself. They included one section of Captain Michael Wiedrich's 1st New York Battery I with two 3" Ordnance Rifles; Captain Hubert Dilger's 1st Ohio Light Battery I with two 12-pounder Napoleons; 4th U. S. Battery G with six 12-pounder Napoleons, commanded by Lieutenant Eugene Bancroft; 1st U. S. Battery H with six 12-pounders, Lieutenant Philip Mason commanding; Captain Wallace Hill's 1st West Virginia Light Artillery, Battery C, with four 10-pounder Parrott Rifles; Lt. George Norton's 1st Ohio Light Battery H, with six 3" Ordnance Rifles, Lieutenant George W. Norton commanding; Captain Frederick M. Edgell's New Hampshire Light, 1st Battery with six 3" Ordnance Rifles; and Capt. Elijah Taft's 5th New York Independent Battery with six large 20-pounder Parrott Rifles.

Hunt spoke with Osborn and Wainwright and learned that everything was quiet and under control. Then, riding west through the Cemetery, he noticed the silent cannons silhouetted against the dawning sky. Osborn's batteries in the Cemetery were pointing west, facing the shadows of Seminary Ridge one mile away, and commanding the approaches through the still darkened fields that lay in between. It was too dark to see any enemy movement.

Hunt had spent much of the early morning of July 3rd riding between Cemetery Hill, the Baltimore Pike, and Meade's headquarters. About 8:00 a.m., heavy skirmishing erupted west of Cemetery Ridge along the Emmitsburg Road, causing Meade a bit of worry. Ordered to check on it, Hunt rode across the Taneytown Road toward Captain John Hazard's II Corps Artillery Brigade, which was posted along north Cemetery Ridge.

It was nearing 9:00 a.m. when Hunt reined to a stop at Lieutenant George A. Woodruff's 1st U. S. Battery I. The six 12-pounders sat unengaged in the open field just west of Ziegler's Grove, with the Emmitsburg Road only 420 feet to their front. Woodruff had allowed his men to go back into the cover of the trees in order to minimize his casualties.

Woodruff's battery anchored the right flank of Major General Winfield Scott Hancock's II Corps. Like Meade and Hunt, Hancock, a 38-year-old Pennsylvanian, was a career army man and commanded his infantrymen with an iron hand. He had graduated from West Point in 1844 and been wounded and brevetted for gallantry in Mexico. At the beginning of the war he found himself in far-off California. Making his way back east, he commanded a brigade in the Peninsula campaign of 1862, and a division at Fredericksburg and Chancellorsville. As a major general, he took command of the II Corps on May 22nd, and upon the death of Major General John Reynolds on July 1st, Meade put him in charge of one wing of the army. He was a tough and disciplined commander but also an effective one, and the enlisted men responded to his efforts with enormous respect. On the field of battle Hancock, usually impeccably dressed in a white dress shirt, seemed to command everything within earshot, whether the troops belonged to him or not. What Hancock did best was fight and get others to fight, and many thought he did that better than any other man on the field.

Subject to incessant skirmishing, Woodruff had already lost two killed and many more wounded. The enemy riflemen had picked off Woodruff's men at such an alarming rate on July 2nd that the battery had been abandoned a few times. Woodruff's casualties were so severe that by dawn on July 3rd, one-third of his battery was manned by infantrymen from Colonel Eliakim Sherrill's 3rd Brigade of Brigadier General Alexander Hays's 3rd Division of the II Corps.

Enemy shells landed sporadically about the ridge as the

sultry morning wore on. Hunt allowed Woodruff to keep under cover as he spurred his horse Bill south along the ridge, parallel to the Emmitsburg Road. Passing the small farm buildings belonging to Abram Bryan, Hunt pulled up at Captain William A. Arnold's 1st Rhode Island Light, Battery A, posted behind a small rock wall two hundred yards south of Woodruff. Arnold's limbers and caissons sat in Bryan's peach orchard on top of the ridge.[10]

As Hunt approached, Arnold was engaged in slow counter-battery fire with a hidden enemy battery posted 1,800 yards to the west on Seminary Ridge. Hunt chastised the captain for wasting ammunition on such targets, telling him that each shot should be fired at identified targets and must have visible results.

To Arnold's immediate left, Lieutenant Alonzo H. Cushing's 4th U. S. Battery A, also with six 3" Ordnance Rifles, was also engaged with the same enemy battery. Cushing sat just west of the ridge. The rock wall in Arnold's front made a 90-degree angle and ran west for 248 feet until it turned back south at what became known as the Angle and continued past the Copse of Trees. Hunt scanned Seminary Ridge and saw the enemy artillery smoke, but not their guns.

Cushing's sergeant, Frederick Fuger, recalled that :

> The morning was all quiet until (approximately) 8:00 a.m. when the enemy opened upon our position, exploding three chests close by.

3 Inch Ordnance Rifle

> General Hunt, Lieutenant Cushing and myself
> were standing close by the number three limber
> when it exploded. General Hunt had marked
> out to me on a piece of paper the directions to
> find the ammunition reserve train. We all
> scattered and the general could not be found.[11]

Hunt, Cushing and Arnold retired to the shelter of the Copse of Trees where Hunt also wrote down the elevation and distance of the enemy battery that was pounding them. He directed his subordinates to limit their fire to proven targets, and not to waste ammunition as it was impractical to engage without seeing results.

The group of officers was joined by Captain John D Hazard, commanding the II Corps Artillery Brigade. He pointed out to Hunt some massed Confederate guns almost a mile away, to the southwest and west of Sherfy's Peach Orchard. Hazard also warned Hunt that Federal skirmishers had heard artillery traffic throughout the night in the swales directly west of the Emmitsburg Road. These Confederate guns were, in fact, waiting for the order from Lee to move forward and engage the Federals. Hunt spoke with Hazard about the condition of his ammunition, telling the captain to draw whatever he needed in preparation for a massed attack. Hazard had done just that the night before. All his batteries sat with packed chests and enough infantrymen on hand to help man the guns.[12]

Hunt left the thickets near the Angle and continued past the batteries of Brown's 1st Rhode Island Light, Battery B, now commanded by Lieutenant Walter Perrin. Perrin had five 12-pounder Napoleons and 97 men. Battery B had been over run the day before and had suffered terribly. Besides two dead, Brown and 20 others had been injured, while many others were simply not fit for combat. Perrin's guns sat just to the left of the Copse of Trees, 60 yards in rear of the same stone wall that crossed Cushing's front, firing toward the William Bliss farm about 600 yards west of the Emmitsburg Road. His solid shot and spherical case slammed into the Bliss orchard as he tried to drive off Confederates holding the farm.

About 150 yards south of Perrin sat the 1st New York Light, Battery B, a unit that had experienced the political forces at work within the army. Initially commanded by Lieutenant Albert Sheldon, when it was transferred out of Brigadier General Robert O. Tyler's Artillery Reserve on July 1st, it reported to

"Gun and Limber"

Hazard for assignment.[13] It was only then that Sheldon learned he had lost command to Captain James M. Rorty.

Rorty had been temporarily assigned to Hazard's staff as chief artillery ordnance officer. Rorty was so good at his job that Hancock took an immediate liking to the captain and dumped the whole II Corps ordnance problem in his lap. Much like Hancock, Rorty was extremely aggressive, conveniently sidestepping military protocol to get what he wanted. When the 14th New York Independent Battery, to which Rorty was assigned, was broken up, two sections went to Ames's 1st New York Light, Battery G, now anchoring McGilvery's left flank. One section of 10-pounder Parrotts was consolidated with Sheldon's 1st New York Light, Battery B and assigned to Hazard's II Corps brigade. In an effort to regain control of his batteries with officers loyal to him, Hancock ordered Hazard to reassign Rorty command of the two 10-pounder Parrotts (from the 14th), thus, by virtue of his rank, giving him command of Sheldon's 1st New York Light, Battery B.[14]

As Hunt rode past Rorty, he was approached by Major General John Newton, commanding the I Corps. The two generals sat for a few moments discussing the day's possibilities. Looking westward toward Seminary Ridge, they could see Confederate cannons being moved into line. Newton had no artillery support to speak of and asked Hunt if some rifled batteries could be spared.[15] Agreeing to supply them as soon as practical, Hunt continued south past Thomas's Battery C and into McGilvery's line. Hunt was impressed with the reserve commander's work. All of McGilvery's batteries then in line were attempting to entrench themselves. Small lunettes of 12 to 18 inches were thrown up in front of each gun, adding a bit of protection.

Hunt and McGilvery watched for a few moments as the fight for the Bliss farm in Hancock's front increased in size, with heavy artillery fire punctuating the solid volleys being traded. Hunt sent aides back to the Artillery Reserve for the batteries General Newton had requested for the I Corps. Hunt told McGilvery not to engage small bodies of men or waste ammunition on batteries too far off, as was happening on

Hancock's line. Hunt cautioned his gunners, stressing that each shot should be deliberate and accurate. McGilvery agreed.[16]

The line McGilvery occupied was an artilleryman's dream. It lay along the west brow of South Cemetery Ridge, facing west by northwest. This position provided a superior line of defensive fire covering much of the area that any attacking Confederate force would have to cross. In addition, guns planted on the "military crest" a few yards west of and below the ridge would have a dark background behind them, making them difficult for enemy artillery to see. Few secondary accounts emphasize the skill shown by Hunt and McGilvery in developing this line.

Cemetery Ridge sloped gently to the west toward a ravine about 400 yards away that paralleled the ridge. Often confused with Plum Run, this ravine angled away from McGilvery's left flank to the northwest toward Plum Run, meeting it on McGilvery's right center just south, and in front of, Thompson's battery. Plum Run was 675 yards west of McGilvery's left flank, about 260 yards farther than the ravine.

A small knoll separated the ravine and Plum Run. This hillock ran almost the entire length of McGilvery's artillery line, parallel to Cemetery Ridge. It masked all but his right two batteries from observation from the west, not only from the Emmitsburg Road but as far as Seminary Ridge. The fields west of Plum Run were dotted with many orchards, farm buildings and various types of wood and rock fences. Federal skirmishers and Berdan's sharpshooters controlled the knoll between the ravines and traded shots with Rebels posted in Trostle's meadows just west of Plum Run. From McGilvery's line itself, there was an unobstructed but limited view to the west as far as Seminary Ridge. Confederates apparently knew little or nothing of the nearly impregnable line of Federal artillery, which was hidden from their view.

Seeing that everything was in order, Hunt again moved south, passing east of the Trostle Woods toward Little Round Top. Two sections of the 1st Ohio Light Battery L, commanded by Lieutenant Frank Gibbs, were posted along the Wheatfield Road on a shelf just west of Cemetery Ridge below and to the north of Little Round Top. One other battery, the 1st New York Light, Battery C, commanded by Captain Almont Barnes, had just pulled out and was moving back over the ridge on the crossroad headed for the Taneytown Road, in rear of the Round Tops. Hunt escorted Barnes a short distance beyond the ridge where the Wheatfield Road crossed over, to the position where Lieutenant Benjamin Rittenhouse's 5th U. S. Artillery Battery D's caissons were in park.

Pennsylvania-born, 24-year-old Benjamin Rittenhouse had assumed command of the battery less than 24 hours earlier as it battled with 5th Corps infantry to retain possession of Little Round Top. Lieutenant Charles Hazlett had led Battery D to Gettysburg, only to be shot through the head as he bent over another wounded officer. Rittenhouse took command and finished the day with an undermanned and severely damaged battery.

Hunt rode up to Little Round Top on the small logging path that scaled its east face. Speaking with Rittenhouse, whose 10-pounder Parrotts were positioned on the west face of the hill, Hunt looked out on the unbroken line of Confederate artillery stretching from the Sherfy Peach Orchard toward the village two miles away. What did it mean?

Hunt then moved off the hill to the north, passing the left section of Gibbs' Battery L. Posted to the right of and below Rittenhouse on the northern-most face of Little Round Top, his two 12-pounders covered the Valley of Death and the Wheatfield. They sat unengaged as their exposed position was hammered by Confederate artillery, drawing much of the fire away from Rittenhouse. Rittenhouse soon opened fire, shooting at anything resembling the enemy beyond the Rose Woods, and drawing return fire. A full 40% of Rittenhouse's men were volunteer infantrymen.[17]

12 Pounderdr Napoleon

Hunt turned east on the Wheatfield Road and continued on to the Taneytown Road east of Cemetery Ridge. From there, he moved north into the Artillery Reserve park, located in the fields belonging to Michael Frey, Sarah Patterson and George Spangler, just east of the road.[18]   The artillery park was a crowded mess.   Hundreds of wagons moved about, as did limbers and caissons. Hospital traffic added to the confusion as wounded were moved into the structures surrounded by the ammunition trains.

Hunt's covert "Ghost Train" was on hand to empty its wagons and make its existence worthwhile.[19] The secret supply train was begun by Hunt in the late fall 1862, while Major General Ambrose Burnside's Army of the Potomac wallowed in the mud around Fredericksburg, Virginia.   With the Grand Divisions into which the army was organized by Burnside much too large to control the river of red tape, Hunt took it upon himself to order goods and equipment, ordnance and quarter-master supplies for his artillery in duplicate and triplicate. Burnside himself supported Hunt's idea of building up the artillery into a self-sufficient fighting force and so ordered his adjutants to help Hunt with whatever he needed.   The commanding officer, of course, never knew of Hunt's over-ordering of supplies.   When Major General Joseph Hooker replaced Burnside in January 1863, things got even easier for Hunt. Demoted to basically a staff position, Hunt had carte-blanche when it came to ordering and demanding immediate supplies.

With Hooker in command, Hunt's beloved artillery was yanked from his immediate command and turned over to the control of the division commanders who would attempt to command batteries from their level, turning the once proud branch of service into a demoralized political mess. Hunt's title of Chief of Artillery became just that, a title.

Hunt believed that control by the division commanders would limit the artillery's use to supporting small units of the army. It would prevent a centralized, professional command with a broader view of any situation from using the guns in the most effective manner, to support the army as a whole, not just its component parts.

Hunt continued to build up his ghost train to a respectable 40 wagons by the time of the battle of Chancellorsville in May, 1863. Calling on Hunt to reorganize the artillery after his defeat at Chancellorsville, Hooker gave Hunt total control

"Caisson and Limber"

to do as he pleased.

Setting aside all personal feelings, Hunt jumped at the task. First he reorganized the batteries, appointing commanders loyal to him and going as far as appointing loyal artillery brigade commanders to be intermediaries between himself and Corps commanders. Gone was the division commanders' hold on the batteries. He organized his well-run reserve brigades plus two reserve brigades of horse artillery, keeping them under lock and key by again appointing tried, veteran commanders selected for their professionalism and loyalty to him.

By June, 1863, Hunt had an efficient, well-run official reserve train equipped to handle anything, as well as the covert reserve train that by now had grown to nearly 60 wagons. Quartermaster General Rufus Ingalls, a personal friend of Hunt, was the only general officer other than Hunt who knew of the covert train's existence. The train itself was staffed by trusted officers who never let their men know of its illegitimacy. None of the private soldiers, guards, escorts or teamsters knew that the equipment they carried was illegal.

The covert train carried foodstuffs, supplies, and more important, about 7,700 rounds of various types of extra ammunition. This averaged out to 20 extra rounds for every cannon assigned to the Army of the Potomac. This was in addition to the 90,000 rounds carried by the regular reserve train and the artillery brigades themselves.

Major General George G. Meade, a 48-year-old Pennsylvanian, had only been in command of the army since June 27th, when President Abraham Lincoln relieved Major General Joseph Hooker. Yet Meade had accomplished much by relying on the words and actions of a few dependable subordinates. Meade had been a career officer, and, like his opponent Robert E. Lee, an excellent engineer. Like Hunt, Meade was a thorough professional and loathed the mistakes and ineptness of politically-appointed officers. He had been seriously wounded in 1862, but quickly returned to duty. On the eve of the battle of Gettysburg he issued a general order that anyone who failed to do his duty in the coming struggle would be executed. Tough as he was, he also was a dedicated family man, and took time nearly every day to write a letter to his wife.

When Meade assumed command of the army, Hunt and Ingalls kept their secret from him.[20] The covert ammunition wagons were brought up and placed in park on the George Spangler farm, emptied their contents and then immediately returned to Westminster, Maryland, the closest operational rail terminal to Gettysburg

Returning to Army headquarters, Hunt was questioned by Meade on the condition of his men and guns, and Meade also expressed concern for the ammunition. Hunt evaded the question by telling his commanding officer that there was ample ammunition on hand and not to worry. Meade asked Hunt to reinspect the line, telling him to place artillery wherever he felt it was most needed.[21]

One More Inspection

About noon, Hunt left Meade's Headquarters for Cemetery Hill. Upon reaching the crest (somewhere around the present day Visitor Center), Hunt looked out over Cemetery Ridge and saw an incredible sight he would remember for the rest of his life:

> Our whole front for two miles was covered by enemy batteries already in line or going into position. They stretched in one unbroken mass from opposite the town, to as far south as the Peach Orchard. Never before on this continent had such a sight been witnessed.[22]

Hunt was still not sure what it meant. He was almost positive that an attack on Cemetery Hill was imminent, but there was the slim possibility that Lee was only planning to cover his withdrawal. Past experiences got the best of Hunt as he spurred Bill across Cemetery Ridge and through Ziegler's Grove; Lee was here to fight.

Moving past Arnold's Battery to the Copse of Trees, Hunt pulled up at Cushing's position. As Hunt, Hazard, Cushing and Arnold stood talking, a shrill whistling was heard followed by a massive explosion. Enemy gunners focused on the Copse of Trees for distance and fired on the mounted officers.

"Withdrawal By Prolonge"

The shells missed the officers but struck several of Cushing's ammunition chests which exploded in a violent ball of flame. The group of men, all visibly shaken, moved back into the Copse of Trees to seek cover. Battery A returned fire, its case shells skyrocketing toward their intended targets along Seminary Ridge, almost one mile away. After warning Hazard again about wasting ammunition, Hunt rode south at a rapid pace.

Passing Perrin and Rorty, Hunt stopped only long enough to warn the two officers about wasting ammunition. He told them that when the Confederate fire opened, they were to wait at least 15 minutes to reply, and then to fire only with slow, deliberate precision. He again repeated his instructions: "Do not waste ammunition uselessly on small bodies of men and artillery that you are not able to see."[23] This was the second time he had directed these instructions to most of Hazard's battery commanders.

As Hunt continued south, he was surprised to see that only one rifled battery had reported to General Newton. Calmly standing near his New York Light, 1st Battery was Capt. Andrew Cowan. Born in Scotland, the 22-year-old Cowan had moved to the U.S. with his parents and was in college when the war broke out. He joined up as an infantry private, but transferred to the artillery and had risen to the command of a battery.

Hunt rode up to Cowan and ordered him to move his battery one hundred yards farther west, below the brow of the crest, just in front of a small cluster of brush and saplings. Hunt and Cowan both rode forward to the main Federal line now only yards in front of the battery. Hunt spoke to Cowan about the type of fire he wanted, telling him as he had told Rorty and Perrin, to wait 15 minutes before opening.

As Hunt turned to ride to McGilvery's line, the 9th

Michigan Battery flew past Cowan's left flank and onto west Cemetery Ridge via the Hummelbaugh farm lane. Captain Jabez J. Daniels led his six 3" rifles by column of sections, using the whip as they came over the ridge, his horse-mounted cannoneers cheering wildly. Motioning with drawn sword, he yelled "Left oblique by section, Reverse trot, Battery." The horse-battery swung around on orders, scattering gawking infantrymen in all directions. Newton was pleased with its arrival, but not impressed with its entrance. Hunt and Doubleday were simply glad to see it.

Detached from Captain James Robertson's 1st Reserve Horse Artillery Brigade, this colorful Englishman-turned-Yank had never before seen battle, and neither had most of his 110 men. Sporting new but dusty uniforms, and sparkling new 3" Ordnance Rifles, the battery was eager for action. Watching them clear the ridge, one would have thought the well-trained and cocky horse cannoneers were crack artillerymen, and they were![24]

Daniels moved his battery into position in the low ground just north of Thomas's 4th U.S Battery C, displacing some of some sharpshooters and infantry. Covered on his right flank by some rough ground and a large Vermont Brigade, Daniels unlimbered. He had a clear field of fire in all directions, but was still low enough not to be seen. His position was possibly the best along all of Cemetery Ridge. Hunt gave Daniels the same orders as everyone else, and then moved on to Thomas's battery on McGilvery's line.

The top layer of soil on Cemetery Ridge was only a few inches deep, and beneath it was loose, but hard, shale. This crumbling rock, present throughout the battlefield, was especially prevalent on Cemetery Ridge, so the men could not dig in. Although Thomas's lunettes were no more than 18" high, he had reinforced his small mounds with wood and stones and was well-entrenched. Standing with Thomas behind his battery was a group of young officers, who stopped talking as Hunt approached and politely acknowledged him with salutes.[25]

Staying mounted, Hunt spoke to the men about the situation at hand. They all knew something big was coming. He reiterated his order on the firing and wished them all luck. At this time McGilvery rode up and entered the conversation, telling Hunt that Dow's 6th Maine Light was back on line. Hunt was glad to hear this and asked McGilvery if he could spare one unit for Hazard, as his II Corps line was spread very thin.

After bidding the men farewell, McGilvery escorted Hunt south down his entrenched artillery line. It was a sight to behold. Upon reaching Ames' Battery G, which was anchoring the left flank, Hunt and McGilvery looked back up the line and decided to send Milton and Turnbull's combined sections north to Hazard. Hunt told McGilvery to send for more reinforcements if necessary, then bid him so long and continued on.

As Hunt moved south to Little Round Top, Col. Warner escorted Milton and Turnbull north up the Taneytown Road. Milton was leading with his section from the 9th Massachusetts, followed by Turnbull's 3rd U. S.[26] After passing Meade's Headquarters, the column probably turned left on the small farm lane leading west up Cemetery Ridge to the Bryan house. (Their path would cut through the present day Cyclorama lobby and entrance.) Pulling into the Bryan farmyard, Brigadier General Henry Baxter, commanding the 2nd Brigade of the 2nd Division of the I Corps took over, placing Milton's two Napoleons just north of the Bryan barn, about seventy-five yards south of Woodruff. Milton unlimbered just west of Ziegler's Grove, his two guns facing across the Emmitsburg Road, which was 475 feet from his muzzles. Turnbull was posted, by General Hays, in the southern part of the Bryan orchard on top of the ridge, with his two Napoleons obliqued (at angles) to the southwest, facing the Angle and the Codori farm beyond. Milton and Turnbull both prepared for action. Milton opened on the Bliss orchard that surrounded the now burning Bliss barn and house.

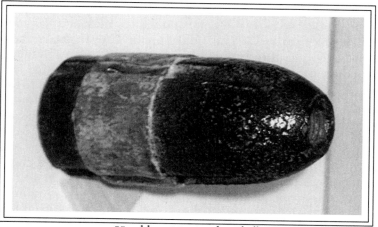

Hotchkiss 10-pounder Shell

The Cannonade

It was now a little before one o'clock. Hunt dismounted on top of Little Round Top, and was impressed at the view before him. The well-placed batteries of both armies sat silent, like predators waiting to pounce. Rittenhouse and Hunt stood talking, while watching the enemy in the Peach Orchard. Rittenhouse pointed out enemy movement past the Peach Orchard toward the Staub farm west of the Emmitsburg Road, in a swale that ran almost perpendicular to Battery D's elevated position. Confederate infantry, laying prone for protection, was massed in close formation. Even from a mile away, it was not hard to see glimmering steel.

As the artillery officers continued talking, a sharp crack, followed a few seconds later by another, ended the waiting. Within three seconds of the second Confederate signal, their whole line exploded in flame. From Little Round Top, the opening spectacle was awesome. Within another few seconds, the entire Confederate line was engulfed in powder smoke, which blocked the enemy batteries from Hunt's view. The hot, still day caused the burning smoke to hang low to the ground, and it concealed most of the batteries. Even from as far away as Battery D's position, one could see brave rebel gunners walking forward through the smoke trying to follow their shots. Fortunately for most Federals on Cemetery Ridge, their aim was terrible. Hunt gave the men on Little Round Top some orders, no doubt pertaining to ammunition, and then climbed down from the crest and mounted his horse.

Hunt spurred Bill north, holding to the ridge. He rode past Ames's Battery G, now sitting under cover in the Weikert Woods. Hunt noticed that more enemy shells were slamming into the woods than into the position that the battery had just left. Hunt rode up to Ames and ordered his guns back out to the ridge. As Hunt continued north he was happy to see that none of McGilvery's gunners had yet opened fire. Hunt then moved east over the ridge toward the Artillery Park.

Most of the enemy shells were passing 40 feet overhead and exploding on top of or behind the crest. Some of these rounds sailed 100 feet over the ridge, landing east of the Taneytown Road. Brigadier General Robert O. Tyler's Artillery Reserve was being pummeled as it sat in the fields about the Taneytown Road. On Hunt's order, Lieutenant Gillette's reserve train was hauled back toward the Baltimore Pike, while the batteries made their way as best they could. It was every battery for itself in the attempt to get out of harm's way.[27]

As instructed, McGilvery's officers waited the full 15 minutes before opening, and those who did, fired slowly and deliberately. A full-scale counter-battery fire from them would simply have shown the enemy their exact positions, bringing on a more accurate barrage. So they chose to sit and watch in the relative safety of their hidden positions, waiting for the rebel infantrymen to show themselves.

Hunt, who was once an artillery instructor, probably chuckled to himself while thinking of all the artillerists he had trained who were now manning Confederate batteries. "Was I that bad of an instructor?" he thought as he rode up the Taneytown Road, dodging solid shot and exploding missiles. At this point, Meade's headquarters was already abandoned, and the occupants had been scattered. Hunt pulled onto the road and sped back south. Riding over the ridge, he reentered McGilvery's line somewhere north of the Hummelbaugh farm. Hunt was approached by McGilvery, and he commended the colonel on the coolness of his battery commanders.[28]

Pulling onto the ridge, but staying in column east of the crest, was the 1st New Jersey Battery B, commanded by Lieutenant Robert Sims. Sims kept his 10-pounder Parrotts well back of the crest, just west of Weikert Woods. His under-manned battery of 94 men was held in reserve, awaiting further orders.[29] Hunt rode north past Thomas's Napoleons which sat unengaged. Daniels' Michiganders fired past the Klingle house and over the Emmitsburg Road. Mounted on his horse, Daniels rode from gun to gun encouraging and rallying his men. The 9th Michigan had now "seen the elephant," a soldier's term for experiencing combat. Obeying Hunt's orders, Daniels slowly answered the Confederate fire. From Thomas' left, Thompson's five rifles opened with deafening blasts that shook the earth. His Pennsylvanians were aiming at Confederate batteries just across the Emmitsburg Road, north of the Klingle farm. Their mark was true, forcing one Confederate battery to pull back and change directions.

Hunt watched the cannonade from Cowan's position. It was now becoming apparent where the Confederate fire was concentrating. Unlike the excited Daniels, Cowan stood, with field glasses in hand, trying to watch each shot through the thickening smoke. Both Hunt and Cowan noted that most of the enemy's fire was directed just north of Cowan's New Yorkers, toward the II Corps line. The ridge about Cowan vibrated and shook with continued explosions, caused mostly by the Federal batteries posted close to the Hummelbaugh farm, and from the Confederate shells exploding in rear of his position. Cowan's projectiles sailed toward Seminary Ridge, causing only slight damage to Rebel batteries. Unbeknownst to Cowan, the real damage he inflicted was to the Confederate infantry that was lying in the Spangler Woods. Cowan fired slowly and deliberately, using shrapnel and case which blew the limbs and bark off trees. The hot, stifling woods were not a safe place to be as the Federal missiles crashed through the canopy overhead and exploded, causing confusion, injury and death.

From Little Round Top, Rittenhouse fired at will into the massed enemy guns, forcing more than one enemy battery to change its direction of fire and to engage him instead of the II Corps line. A Confederate officer referred to Rittenhouse's battery as "the battery on the mountain."[30] Rittenhouse had done his job very well. His fire would have been considered successful if even one Rebel gun was forced to face about, thereby taking pressure off Hancock's line. He also enfiladed the Confederate infantry lying in the swales. His ricocheting shells landed and bounded down their lines, exploding with telling effect. The heat must have soared above 100 degrees in the bottoms of the small valleys, making the Confederate infantrymen's ordeal even worse.[31]

Hunt left Cowan and rode the gauntlet north toward Hazard's II Corps line. Lieutenant Gulian Weir, one of the small group of officers with whom Hunt had spoken a few minutes earlier at Thomas's battery, rode east over the ridge to the six Napoleons of his 5th United States Artillery Battery C. As Weir cleared the ridge, he noticed a panic. "Men, horses, mules and wagons were moving everywhere, at top speed. Enemy shells plowed the earth and exploded to the point that nowhere was safe." Weir rode into his battery, and ordered a bugler to call "Assembly," "To Horse," and then "Cannoneers Mount." One Rebel shell exploded to the right of the first gun, wounding Lieutenant Homer Baldwin as the column began to move.[32] Baldwin quickly bandaged his wound, procured a sergeant's horse, and rode off after his unit, leaving the sergeant to scurry for cover on foot. Moving through fields under extreme fire, Weir recrossed the Taneytown Road and moved up the ridge via the Hummelbaugh farm lane.

Weir led his smoothbores over the crest to a spot on

Cowan's left flank, and reported to General Newton. The feisty Newton thanked and dismissed Weir, telling the lieutenant that he needed rifles, not 12-pounder smoothbores. Weir's six Napoleons were moved back over the ridge and went into park, in column, facing due north just below the east brow of Cemetery Ridge, very near the Hummelbaugh house, due east of Cowan. Weir himself stayed at Cowan's side watching the cannonade.

Hunt moved from battery to battery in Hazard's II Corps command, encouraging the men as he went. It was pandemonium as shot, shell and case blew the ridge to bits. Caissons, dead horses and mutilated men littered the ground.

"The Guidon"

One gun from the 1st New York Battery B was disabled, and Capt. Rorty was seriously wounded, hit by a fragment from an explosion caused by a direct hit on one of his gun limber chests. Being the veteran that he was, Lt. Sheldon had the mortally wounded Rorty removed and took command, continuing the fight with his three remaining Parrott Rifles. Perrin's 1st Rhode Island Battery B was becoming a mess, as was Cushing's 4th U. S. Battery A. The Copse of Trees was the focal point of the Confederate cannonade, and the nearby gunners were experiencing its full effect.[33]

Yet Confederate fire overshot its target here as well, causing more problems east of the ridge than west of it. As a result, Meade's headquarters, 1,350 feet beyond the Angle, had to be vacated. Hunt moved past Arnold, whose caissons were being blown to bits as they sat in the Bryan orchard. Further on, Turnbull calmly sat on his horse, watching his 3rd U. S. Regulars work his two 12-pounders, firing over Hays' infantry in the front. Hunt crossed behind the Bryan barn, went past Milton's guns, and rode up to Woodruff's Battery I. Hunt spoke to almost every battery commander as he passed, again warning them to take their time and conserve ammunition as things would get worse. From Daniels on the left, past Cowan and north to Woodruff, Hancock's II Corps line was supported by 42 cannons of various types, more than enough if handled correctly.

Hunt lingered a few moments at Woodruff's position, watching the screaming bolts fired from the Confederate's Whitworth rifles on Oak Hill pass overhead. They flew by harmlessly, but with a frightening sound, over Ziegler's Woods and exploded among the noncombatants beyond. The woods were a smoky nightmare as Rebel shells poured into the small grove. The infantry hugging the ground nearby felt the same anxiety as the Confederate infantry in the woods a mile to the west.

From Rittenhouse's position on Little Round Top, north to Woodruff's at Ziegler's Grove, 87 Federal cannons fired from Cemetery Ridge. They caused significant damage to Lee's infantry, which was preparing to charge. The Southern artillerists fared no better. Confederate fire was erratic to begin with, and after the Federals opened, it became even less effective. The Federals had far superior cannons and ordnance, not to mention the inside elevated line which allowed their artillery to be replaced within minutes. They were, in fact, the better artillerists. Lee had under his command some of the best trained and schooled artillery commanders in either army, some from West Point, but most from the Virginia Military Institute. All were brave and determined commanders, but they could not match the professionalism and skill of the Federal gunners. And the men of Hunt's well-trained and organized artillery officer's corps were turning out to be just as brave and determined.

Meade's Headquarters and Cemetery Hill

When the cannonade commenced, General Meade had ridden east to Power's Hill and established his temporary headquarters near Maj. Gen. Slocum's XII Corps headquarters.[34] No one knew where he was, and he must have felt uneasy about the lack of correspondence and communication he was receiving at his new headquarters. Confederate projectiles fired from north of the town landed very close to Slocum's command post along the Baltimore Pike.

Federal artillery on top of and below Power's Hill, as well as on McAllister's Hill, were engaged to the east as Rebel troop movement across Rock Creek was detected. This, in fact, was a reconnaissance in force by Walker's Stonewall Brigade of Johnson's Division. The brigade, ordered to see if the Federal far right could be breached, moved out through the woods skirting Rock Creek. Their movement was slowed by the Federal artillery, hammering the thick woods.

The din was all too much for Meade. After remounting Baldy, the general rode north up the Baltimore Pike, dodging rebounding shot and exploding shells. As Meade rode through the Evergreen Cemetery gate, he yelled, "Maj. Osborn! Where is Maj. Osborn?" Meade had noticed the high rate of artillery fire and was visibly upset. Osborn called out to Meade from the area just east of the Cemetery, "Over here, General." Meade rode up to the dismounted major, and asked him, "Don't you know that it is against general orders and military regulations to run out of ammunition during a battle." Osborn was stunned, but replied, "I never gave it much thought." A simple answer for one as busy as he. Meade went on, "What do you intend to do at this position?" Osborn replied, "I will hold this position if the infantry supports me." Meade looked about, saying, "I don't think you will hold this position, but, since you intend to stay, watch your fire and make every shell count. Call on the reserve if you need ammunition."[35]

Osborn's gunners skillfully worked their pieces as Confederate fire began to take its toll. Hill's 1st West Virginia Battery C was hammered as it was hit from the southwest, west, northwest, and north. The batteries were so crowded on the western crest of Cemetery Hill that, in some places, each gun

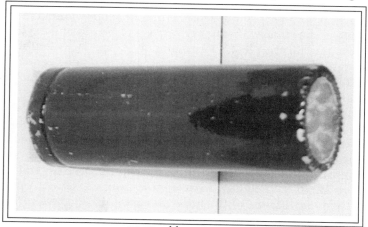

3" Hotchkiss Canister

stood only 10 feet apart, which made walking from battery to battery almost impossible. The powder-smoke hung on the hill, choking the men and stinging their eyes. The young cannoneers, some with rolled-up shirt sleeves, others bare-chested, served their pieces as smoke and grime turned their sweat-soaked bodies black. Osborn walked his line giving orders and directing fire, encouraging his gunners to stand tall and "take your time and feed it to 'em."[36] A huge explosion along the Baltimore Pike startled Osborn as one of Taft's 20-pounder Parrotts exploded, killing two men and seriously wounding six others. Taft cleared the debris, pulled the disabled piece out of line, and continued his battle against Benner's Hill as if nothing had happened.

Just west of Cemetery Hill, Hunt rode east from Woodruff's position through Ziegler's Grove. He crossed the Taneytown Road and rode up Cemetery Hill toward Osborn's command. Upon entering the Cemetery, Hunt spied the XI Corps artillery commander. Dismounting, Hunt walked west with Osborn to the center of the Cemetery. While talking over the situation, Hunt and Osborn were joined by Major General Oliver O. Howard, commander of the XI Corps, and one of his division commanders, Major General Carl Schurz.

The four officers talked as the Confederate fire seemed to intensify around the Cemetery. It was equal to that along Cemetery Ridge. Although inaccurate, some Confederate rounds did find their mark. One solid shot plowed into six horses standing just a few yards from the group of officers. All six animals were killed or mortally wounded on the spot. The three generals simply looked over their shoulders and continued to talk as if it had not happened.[37] Another shell bounded in rear of one of the stone walls that crisscrossed the hill and exploded in the middle of a New York regiment, killing or wounding 30 men. When the colonel of the stricken regiment requested permission to move, Howard told him to stay put, as moving would display cowardice to others. Howard was as brave as anyone on that hill.[38]

The four officers continued talking, speculating about Lee's objective, and came to the consensus that Lee intended to attack the heights and cut the Federal line in half. Unbeknown to them, that was exactly Lee's plan. When Osborn asked Hunt what Meade's thoughts were on the subject, Hunt replied, "Meade had expressed the hope that they would attack."[39]

As Hunt talked to the officers on Cemetery Hill, about one mile south of them a significant event took place. Hancock and McGilvery got into a heated argument near McGilvery's line. Riding into McGilvery's line Hancock ordered all the right flank batteries he came upon to open fire. Cowan, Daniels, Thomas and Thompson complied with the order, Hart and Phillips did not. Hart argued with Hancock that he had received not only orders from McGilvery, but also from Hunt. Both had told him to delay his fire. Raging with profanity Hancock threatened both captains with arrest. Only then did they order their guns to open.[40]

McGilvery heard the reports from the now active guns. Deciding to investigate, he spurred his horse toward a group of officers behind Hart's battery. Dismounting, McGilvery confronted Hancock by telling Capt. Hart to cease fire. Being a retired sea captain, McGilvery's oaths and profanity were equal to Hancock's. Reminding the general that he had no authority

"Fire!"

over the reserve guns, McGilvery finished the conversation by telling Hancock where he could go.[41] But the damage was done. McGilvery's line was now being hit much harder than before Hancock's order. His right flank was far more exposed than his left. The low open crest behind the line of guns became a hell as Confederate batteries, still overshooting their intended targets, pummeled the crest where the limber and caissons sat in park. Thompson's Pennsylvanians were being pounded by a Confederate battery that had run two 20-pounder Parrott rifles east of the Emmitsburg Road and northeast of the Klingle barn. The Confederates had Thompson in perfect enfilade from only 900 yards, and they had the advantage of a slight elevation. Thompson reeled at the nearly point-blank fire as the enemy gunners poured in case and shell. Long distance canister was even fired as the brave Rebel gunners pushed their rifled pieces closer.

Two of Thompson's rifles were struck and put entirely out of action. He fought on with his remaining three guns. Clearly, the Confederates were getting the best of him. A dozen of his horses were down, with no more fresh ones to spare. Ten men and four officers were also down, including Lieutenant Joseph Miller. Hit by shrapnel, the young officer died from his wounds on August 9th. McGilvery proceeded to order some of his rifled batteries to reopen slowly, concentrating their fire on single targets.[42]

The Lure

It was during the conversation between Hunt, Osborn, Howard and Schurz on Cemetery Hill that the idea of encouraging the Confederates into a premature charge was probably born. Osborn suggested that a reduction of artillery fire from the Federal lines might lure the Confederates into an attack into the face of a well-prepared and destructive artillery fire. Hunt and Osborn *wanted* Lee to charge, and sought to lure Lee into it. Osborn recalled:

> I said to these officers that I believed that if we should stop firing along our entire line suddenly and as though the artillery on Cemetery Hill was driven off the field, Lee would at once develop his plans—that if the General would give me permission, I would stop my batteries at once. Hunt said that he thought I was correct, and if Howard agreed to it, he would give the order. Howard thought the suggestion a good one and said that he would like to see the experiment tried... [Hunt] then gave the order to stop firing and said that he would ride down the line and stop all the batteries.[43]

Meade, Osborn, Howard and Hunt had come to the same conclusion. Their guns would be silenced for two purposes: to save ammunition for the Charge, and to convince the Confederates to begin.

Hunt asked Osborn the same question Meade had asked: "If you stopped your fire, would your men stay here?" Osborn said that they would if they received infantry support. Hunt, like Meade, expressed doubts about the infantry's willingness to stay. Having heard enough of this, Howard interrupted Hunt, saying, "I support Maj. Osborn's idea of stopping the artillery fire, and my men will stay!"[44]

They agreed that Osborn would take charge on the hill and tell Wainwright of the plan, and Hunt would make sure all the batteries along Cemetery Ridge would cease firing. As Hunt remounted Bill, he politely asked General Howard to make sure that Meade received word of their plan, just in case he could not find the commanding officer himself. Howard agreed, sending couriers off to find the commanding general, whose own couriers were searching for Hunt with the same message.[45]

Osborn set out immediately to stop his own and Wainwright's batteries. The order was to slow down, and then, within a few minutes, cease fire altogether. Osborn's command was spread across Cemetery Hill, facing west to northwest. Its

"Defend the Gun"

left flank was anchored on a little knoll just south of Cemetery Hill and east of the current Visitor's Center parking lot. There sat Lieutenant George Norton's 1st Ohio Battery H, facing due west. A small copse of woods to his left rear concealed most of his caissons. Norton's six rifles fired into McMillan's Woods on Seminary Ridge. His gunners endured a crossfire that, fortunately, killed no one. Norton was the first to cease fire, securing his pieces by pulling them back into the small wood.[46]

Captain Frederic M. Edgell's 1st New Hampshire Light, posted in a corn field east of the knoll and facing northeast, also ceased fire. Edgell received an order from Osborn to pull his six rifles back to the left of Hill's 1st West Virginia Battery C, facing due west. Edgell did this as Confederate fire continued its barrage onto the hill.[47]

Hill engaged enemy batteries south of the Lutheran Seminary, forcing one of them to pull back to a safer position.

To Hill's right was Lt. Philip Mason's 1st U. S. Battery H. Mason's six Napoleons fired over a sunken road and into the fields beyond. He had many targets to chose from. At times, he engaged Rebels who dared show themselves along the sunken road, due west.

After Mason came Bancroft, Dilger and Wiedrich. All three of these XI Corps units engaged Confederate batteries directly west of the town along east Seminary Ridge. Most of the Confederate shell that struck the cemetery landed with little physical damage to batteries or personnel. The infantry regiments scattered about bore the brunt of the enemy fire, as did the noncombatants south of the hill, along the Baltimore Pike.

Taft's two west-facing 20-pounder Parrotts were pulled back from Osborn's line and parked along the Baltimore Pike, just opposite and below the corn field. Three of Taft's remaining guns were run due west through the cemetery, to the crest of Cemetery Hill, which had an unobstructed view to the southwest down the Emmitsburg Road.[48] Their exact position is unknown, but it is very possible that they were run into the gap between Hill's left and Edgell's right.[49]

In preparation for the expected infantry attack, Osborn also brought up Lieutenant James Stewart's three serviceable Napoleons of the 4th U. S. Battery B, placing them in line to the right of Dilger, facing west.

Moments prior to Pickett's advance, Maj. Thomas Osborn had 41 cannons of various types pointed west southwest and ready for action. The gunners and cannoneers now hugged the ground, as they had all ceased fire. The Rebel fire continued unabated, but erratic, as the hot afternoon wore on.[50] Osborn was forced to pull Taft's three 20-pounder Parrotts out of the west-facing line and run them north to engage enemy batteries firing from north of the town. The Confederate enfilading fire caused much damage to Osborn's batteries, as well as the infantry. Taft's guns were moved back as soon as the threat was over.

Cemetery Ridge

While Osborn fretted over his batteries, Hunt galloped southwest out of the Cemetery toward Lt. Turnbull's 3rd U. S. Consolidated Battery sitting in the Bryan orchard, with only enough men left to fire one gun. Hunt stopped for a moment to speak with his subordinate about the cease fire, then spurred Bill on, passing Arnold's and Cushing's wrecked caissons in rear of the ridge.[51]

Out of Hunt's line of sight, Cushing stood by his guns, hunched over, grasping his bloody midsection. Hit in the abdomen by a shell fragment, he continued to command his three serviceable rifles on top of the crest. Dead horses and wounded men lay about his line among disabled cannons, limbers, and caissons. Debris from the once proud battery littered the position, and still, the enemy fire continued, with no sign of letting up.

As Hunt rode along Cemetery Ridge, one of Hancock's staff officers, Captain Henry Bingham, was looking for him, with a written order from Meade. The order stated that either Hunt or Hancock should "see that their batteries take care with their ammunition and endeavor to preserve it and not fire so rapidly or extravagantly." Not finding Hunt or Hancock, Bingham proceeded on his own with the order to each battery commander north of the thickets, including Cushing, and ordered them to do just what Hunt wanted them to do.[52]

As Hunt passed the crest somewhere east of the Copse of Trees, the first battery he came upon was Perrin's 1st Rhode Island Light, Battery B, sitting, virtually destroyed, just south of the Copse of Trees. Hunt ordered the battery out, and the wounded Perrin assembled his men under fire to begin a not-so-orderly withdrawal. As they slowly pulled back, while enemy shells continued to hammer the Federals near the Angle, the

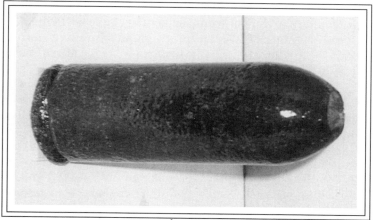

10 pounder Parrott Shell

departing gunners saw glimmering steel move out from the woods a mile away to the west.[53]

Moving farther south, Hunt pulled up to the 1st New York Battery B, now commanded by Lieutenant Robert Rogers. It was here that Hunt learned of Rorty's death, and of the wounding of Rorty's subordinate, Lt. Sheldon. When asked what he intended to do, Rogers replied, "I'll hold my ground."[54] Hunt told him to consolidate his three pieces into two, probably due to the lack of both men and ammunition. Rogers saluted and began one of the finest battery stands at Gettysburg. Rogers pushed two serviceable Parrotts toward the small stone wall, forcing his guns between the left of the 19th Maine and the right of the 15th Massachusetts. The artillerymen and infantry volunteers stacked all the canister, and what shell they had left, in between the guns. Then, as ordered by Hunt, they took refuge behind the stone wall with the infantry.

Hunt then proceeded to Cowan's position, admiring the battery as he approached. Cowan's men stood to their pieces, moving through their drill with quick motions, but taking time to be sure all was right. Newton intercepted Hunt, and again pleaded for more artillery, pointing past the Vermont Brigade and stating, "I need more rifles to cover this gap." Hunt asked for a volunteer and sent several of Cowan's men to Tyler for reinforcements. Unknown to Hunt, Doubleday had already sent several aides, and support was already on its way. Hunt then continued south.[55]

Hunt's order to cease fire made Hancock furious. He had not taken part in the discussions, had not received the order from Meade, and did not want the artillery to cease firing. The II Corps commander was an infantryman's infantryman: he wanted the artillery to continue firing to boost his men's morale and to do whatever damage it could.

Thus Hancock rode along his entire battle line following Hunt by a few minutes, issuing orders to II Corps batteries to resume their fire. Capt. John Hazard, Hancock's own artillery commander, disagreed with Hancock, telling him that Hunt had issued the correct order.[56] Hancock would not hear of this and ordered Hazard to reopen with rapid fire. Hazard sent out orders to the batteries that Hancock had not reached and the Federal guns on north Cemetery Ridge were once again covered in their own smoke.

Unknown to Hunt, Hancock continued south down the line ordering even the reserve batteries not attached to Hazard's

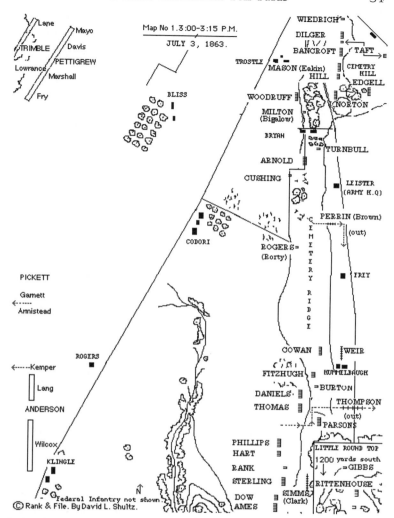

Map No 1. 3:00-3:15 P.M.
JULY 3, 1863.

brigade to open as well. Hancock gave direct orders for Cowan, Daniels and Thomas to reopen at once. Not venturing into McGilvery's line after the earlier altercation with the Lieutenant Colonel, Hancock turned back and disappeared north into the smoke.

McGilvery's Line

When Hunt reached McGilvery's reserve line, not yet realizing Hancock had earlier rebuked the colonel, Hunt repeated the message to cease fire and prepare for infantry. As he passed Thomas's six smoking Napoleons, he was shocked to see Thompson's decimated battery, still holding its position with three rifles. Addressing Thompson, Hunt learned of Hancock's order and of Thompson's duel with the Confederate battery, now under cover of the Klingle Barn. Looking over the mess, Hunt ordered Thompson out, telling him to see that Tyler sent up a replacement right away. McGilvery was now next to Hunt, excitedly telling him about Hancock's order. After reassuring Hunt that enough ammunition was on hand for the coming infantry attack, McGilvery suggested that an order be sent to call up the remaining reserves. Hunt told him that more guns were on the way and then thanked McGilvery for his actions. Hunt was satisfied with McGilvery's artillery line. He and McGilvery then continued down the line to the position of Ames's 1st New York Battery G, which was still anchoring the left flank.

While Hunt talked with McGilvery, an orderly rode up with the order from Meade to discontinue firing. Learning that the order was already being obeyed, the aide rode away. At this time, both Hunt and McGilvery noticed a change in the Confederate fire. Although still heavy, it had a sporadic crack to it as it diminished in volume.

Hunt's trained ear picked up another change. Within minutes after the Federal artillery slowed its fire, a volley of rapid exchanges along the II Corps line told the story. Hazard's batteries had reopened. Although severely wounded, and with a nearly disabled battery, Cushing fought on with his remaining serviceable rifles, ramming home the last shells and sending them westward. Arnold, Woodruff, and Rogers (Rorty) were no better off, and Perrin (Brown) was beginning to pull out. Milton and Turnbull waited, with just enough ammunition for several long range volleys. All of the II Corps batteries on Cemetery Ridge were now running low on long range ammunition.

Hunt rode north at top speed reissuing the order to all the batteries to again cease fire, cease fire! From Ames north to Cowan, all adhered and secured their pieces. Venturing only as far north as the two Parrotts of Rogers' 1st New York Battery B, Hunt turned back in disgust. Rogers had done the unthinkable: he had used up nearly all his long range ammunition. Hunt was too upset to stay on the scene as Rogers' gunners restacked the few case and canister tubes near the Parrotts. Rogers' two guns were sitting some 20 feet east of the stone wall; they had recoiled without being pushed forward.

Dismounting at Cowan's battery, Hunt was joined by two officers.[57] They stood talking as a rustle among Cowan's gunners caught their attention. Barely visible through the smoke to the west, the dark line that Hunt had expected was emerging out of the woods and entering the open, but undulating plain. Moving to align their ranks, the lines of Confederate infantry appeared to run as far north as the eye could see. To the south, the lines disappeared in the swales west of the Emmitsburg Road.

Lieutenant Augustin Parsons led his 1st New Jersey Light, Battery A out of the artillery park and up the east face of Cemetery Ridge at top speed, followed by Captain Robert Fitzhugh's 1st New York Light, Battery K, with the 11th New York under Captain John E. Burton temporarily attached. As they crested the ridge, Parsons' six rifles and caissons temporarily became airborne, with his cannoneers and gunners atop the chests holding on for dear life. Moving past Cowan's left flank, Parsons was picked up by McGilvery, who pointed to Thompson's former position, now filling up with Federal infantry. Confederate shells still landed on the ridge, making Parsons' entrance uncomfortable.

"Column left, reverse trot, forward into battery" was the order. The bugler sounded the call and Parsons' six 3" rifles unlimbered on the west brow of Cemetery Ridge, in rear of Thompson's former position, directly west of the present day Pennsylvania Monument. There was no specific order to the regiments as the infantrymen moved off the crest into the gap.[58]

Parsons, at best, had a limited field of fire over this line of infantry as the ridge here was lower than anywhere else along its length. Fitzhugh, talking with Hunt, motioned with a wave of his arm. Two rifles swung off the lane to their left onto Cemetery Ridge and went into action just south of the Hummelbaugh farm lane, followed by one section that went into the lane and a third that dropped trail to the right of the lane.[59]

As the Confederate infantry stepped out of the shadows of the Spangler Woods nearly one mile west of the Copse of Trees, an officer in the 8th Virginia looked up and down the line.:

> The division moved forward at command, in common time, and it cleared the woods, its work was seen before it. Long lines of bristling

bayonets and blackened mouths of numerous artillery, which at this time were quietly awaiting to deal death and destruction to us.[60]

The first guns to fire on the Confederate infantry from Cemetery Hill began shelling the massing Confederate lines.[61] Rittenhouse, who had not received Hunt's order, had never stopped firing from Little Round Top. It was about 3:00 p.m.[62]

The Charge

Virtually all Federal batteries facing west reopened, save the II Corps. In his official report, Capt. John Hazard stated, "All my batteries sat idle until the Rebel lines were halfway across the field."[63] Lacking long-range ammunition, his gunners had stacked their canister at their guns and waited. To their right on Cemetery Hill, the roar was unbearable as the batteries fired at will. The Confederate artillery, in a vain attempt to silence the Federal batteries and draw attention away from their infantry, still fired wildly over the hill. "The gunners on Cemetery Hill concentrated on the Confederate line now advancing," recalled Osborn, "paying no attention at all to the enemy batteries still firing."[64]

Watching his fire from inside the Cemetery, Osborn was told by someone that one of his batteries was dumping ammunition into the small wood just east of the little knoll south of Cemetery Hill. Walking behind his line, Osborn approached Edgell's New Hampshire Battery. From afar, Osborn spied Norton's Ohio Battery fleeing down the Taneytown Road toward the artillery park. Osborn spotted ammunition abandoned on the ground east of the little knoll, but there was no time to worry about this.[65] He had more important things to do. Norton's was the first and only intact Federal battery to pull out of position during the Confederate advance. Why Norton chose to leave will never be known. Perhaps, like many others on Cemetery Hill, the men from Ohio believed that the attack was headed for them, and it appeared through the smoke and confusion that the seemingly endless enemy lines just might reach them.

What Osborn needed now was another battery to cover his left flank. He sent a message for help to Col. Wainwright, and the I Corps artillery commander responded by sending one section of Ricketts' 1st Pennsylvania Light, and one section of

Wiedrich's 1st New York. Ricketts personally led two rifled cannons across the Baltimore Pike and into the cornfield south of the Cemetery, placing the guns to the southeast of the little knoll. He would be reinforced with two more pieces by the time Pickett was repulsed.[66] Opening on the Confederate left with percussion shells and case, Ricketts had a beautiful field of fire along the entire line. The small woods on Ricketts' right front gave him some flanking cover and security as his own rounds sailed over the Taneytown and Emmitsburg Roads. (His present-day field of fire would have been west over the Cyclorama lobby and offices.) Weidrich's center section crossed over the pike and joined his left section in battery north of Dilger.

A few yards northwest of Ricketts, Captain Hill's West Virginians opened, with telling effect, down the Rebel left flank, as did Edgell. Both batteries fired percussion shells from about 1,200 yards away, at left oblique to the attacking column. It would have been hard for them to miss. Hill watched his exploding shells slam into the exposed line, opening visible gaps that closed quickly.

The percussion shells from all of Osborn's rifled batteries slammed into the Confederate ranks, detonating on impact and sending torn bodies flying. The solid shot from the smoothbores bounded and ricocheted through the lines with devastating physical and mental effects. But the huge holes opened by both shot and shell blasts closed up, and the ranks moved on. The timed-fuse shells, fired just to the front of the advancing columns, exploded as the lines neared or passed over them.

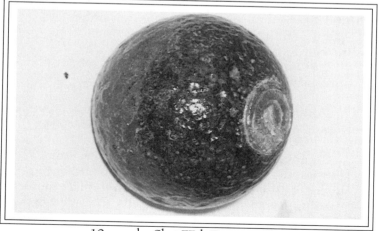

12 pounder Shot With Bormann Fuse

Again, the damage was frightful. Confederate infantry began to quit in small droves, increasing in numbers as the lines advanced. Case—a thin-walled projectile, filled with musket balls, that exploded by a timed fuse—was the real killer as its pre-impact explosion spewed shrapnel and fragments over a wide area.

Soon a steady stream of wounded, and non-wounded as well, began to turn back as the Federal artillery pummeled the lines. Yet Edgell reported that the lines he fired on, although cut to pieces, closed up to their right and moved on.

Captain Taft's three 20-pounder Parrotts rained havoc on the far-left brigade of the enemy line. Taft stated in his writings, "I could sight down the entire length of their line, which stretched as far south as the eye could see, a perfect enfilading shot for my gunners . . . I watched my fire stop and break one column, all the men turning back in mass seeking cover in the woods."[67] The already decimated Confederates fell in rows as they angled to the southeast, offering the Federal gunners on Cemetery Hill their left shoulders.

Mason's Napoleons fired to the west, as did Bancroft's, Stewart's, Dilger's and Weidrich's four rifles. Stewart described his fire on the Confederate lines:

> As Pickett's lines advanced toward the Emmitsburg Road and pressed up the slope, the Rebel infantry in our front began to advance. Their left flank reaching very near the southern edge of town, in fact their extreme left was entering the streets . . . We now got orders to open on them with spherical case, to bear on their left as far as we could, without shelling the town itself. We fired slowly several rounds, but as the enemy halted again we ceased.

He finished by saying, "Our practice was very good; every one of our case shot struck home and exploded in their ranks."[68]

Shrapnel screamed over and down the Emmitsburg Road, toward the Confederate's left flank. Solid shot from the 12-pounder batteries bounded and bounced through the Rebel lines, causing more damage than the shells. The effect of these solid shots was extremely demoralizing for the infantrymen. As the line neared the smoldering Bliss buildings, the number of men leaving the ranks seemed to markedly increase. Still, for the most part, the lines moved on with great coolness.[69] Yet at one time during the Charge, one regiment had to fix bayonets to stop overwhelming numbers of stragglers from plowing through their own ranks.[70]

Osborn now had 41 cannons firing at left enfilade down the left flank of the Confederate line. They pummeled the Confederates so hard that a general move by the Rebel line to the south was initiated from the sheer instinct to survive. The men on the far left began to crowd to the right, forming small groups, which allowed for even more casualties as they continued on. Not only were Virginians leaving the field on the far left, but men from Mississippi, North Carolina, and Alabama were dropping back as well. If Malvern Hill or Antietam was artillery hell, then what the Confederate infantry walked into at Gettysburg on July 3rd may never be accurately described in words.

Concerning the artillery's execution from Cemetery Hill, Osborn said it best:

> By watching the effects of their fire the gunners soon had the exact range. The smoothbores fired solid shot and the rifles percussion shell, this was changed accordingly. Each solid shot or unexploded shell cut out at least two men. The exploding shells took out four, six, eight men, sometimes more than that, with twice that many turning back.[71]

Lieutenant Frederick Edgell watched the good work his New Hampshire cannoneers were doing as their projectiles enfiladed the Confederate flank:

> A grand attack was made by the enemy . . . and I commenced a rapid fire of case shot on . . . his advancing lines. I fired obliquely from my position upon the left of the attacking column with destructive effect, as that wing was broken and fled in confusion across the fields back into the woods.

He went on to explain that his battery expended 248 rounds of shell and case against these attacking lines, all within one hour.[72]

Below Cemetary Hill one Confederate officer noted the effectiveness of the artillery fire:

> Our troops marched over open fields, exposed at every step to a most destructive [artillery] fire, for a mile. This distance broke down the men and exhausted the ranks, which thinned. They only reached the enemy lines in small numbers and were repulsed. The error was in charging over so broad a space. Had the troops been marched to within one half mile of the Federal works at night, and charged vigorously at day-break we might have carried the enemy line.[73]

The last statement explains how crucially important it was to control the William Bliss house and barn, about half way between the lines. Whoever possessed it had a most definite advantage. The swale just east of the buildings sat well below the brow of Cemetery Hill, out of Osborn's field of fire. This would have given the Confederates some protection before starting their charge, and reduced the time they were under severe artillery fire.

Little Round Top

As Osborn's gunners opened from Cemetery Hill, Rittenhouse continued his terrific enfilading fire from the "mountain." As a result, when the men on the right flank of Pickett's line rose to their feet in the swale south of the Spangler farm, at least 300 casualties stayed put. Some of this damage had been done by McGilvery's line, especially by the rifled batteries, but most had been done by Rittenhouse.

The Confederate far-right was being hit as hard as the far-left of the line, and the right had a long way to go under this grueling fire, much further than those under fire from Cemetery Hill. The right flank of the Confederate infantry would, in fact, attack up the Emmitsburg Road after crossing to the east, offering its right and back to Rittenhouse as it moved almost due north.

As the right flank brushed past the Klingle farm, with

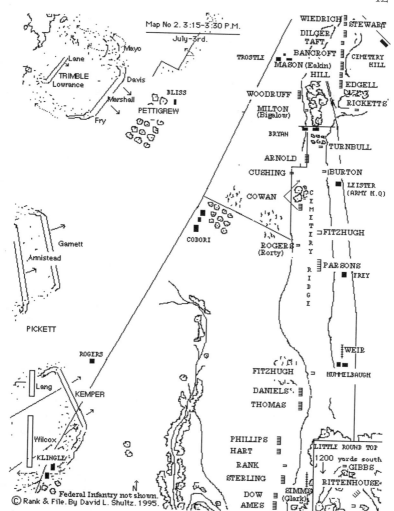

several companies passing to the south, it immediately began to descend into the Plum Run valley. Rittenhouse continued to pound the Confederate right rear with devastating effect. One round from "the mountain" took out 30 men as it tumbled down the line from right to left and exploded.

McGilvery's Line

As the Confederate infantry moved into Plum Run it executed a difficult left-oblique maneuver. This entire move was done under devastating flank-fire from Fitzhugh's center section and Thomas's, Daniels', and Parsons' batteries. The right flank of the Confederate line was becoming completely unmasked as it moved north of the small hill that separated Plum Run from the ravine. Yet the Rebels continued moving due north, passing McGilvery's line, which sat facing west-northwest. They were completely exposed, and all of McGilvery's batteries pounded them unmercifully.

With spectacular execution, Ames, Dow, Sterling, Rank, Hart and Phillips poured it on. Their combined 28 pieces fired anything their tubes could handle. Ames' Napoleons fired case and solid shot at the Confederate rear from only 800 yards away. Sterling's two large-bored 12-pounder Howitzers fired spherical case, tearing huge openings in the line. Sterling's large bronze rifles fired shell and canister, as did Rank's two 3" rifles. Hart's and Phillip's gunners worked like mad men, hitting the enemy line with case and canister at only 400 yards. McGilvery's line was actually forcing the Confederates north, transforming the line into a massive mob bearing little resemblance to an attacking line. The surviving Confederates, for the most part, simply lowered their heads and moved on, yet hundreds, wounded and unwounded, quit the field and moved back west.[74]

The Emmitsburg Road offered a brief respite to many of these once-brave infantrymen in gray, who now refused to go forward. Unlike at Malvern Hill in 1862, the men knew the futility of such an attack against semi-fortified infantry positions with strategically placed artillery packed nearly hub to hub. The center of the right flank came into point-blank range of Fitzhugh's, Thomas's and Daniels' guns, who showed no mercy. Thomas calmly stood at his right gun, watching as the enemy line was hammered to the north.[75]

Daniels continued with shell, case, and canister, switching to double canister as the line moved past. The large Vermont Brigade to his right stood and fired long distance volleys as the Confederates crossed into their front. Fitzhugh's center section continued to fire timed-case from its position above the Vermont Brigade. Along the entire line, thousands of Confederates were now moving back across the Emmitsburg Road. But what remained of their lines still closed up toward the center and moved on.

As the Confederate line moved north, a strange thing happened along McGilvery's line. Several Federal infantry regiments pulled out of Thompson's vacated position and moved north. Some individuals moved by themselves, while others moved as whole units. In fact, the entire line began following the Confederate line. Slowly they moved north toward the Copse of Trees. They would squeeze into openings between batteries, fire, and then step back, load, and fire again.[76]

By the time the attacking line moved past Thomas's position, hundreds of mixed Federal infantrymen were moving in mass, firing, loading, moving and firing again. More than once, Daniels had to cease fire to clear his front. It was as if a giant, violent parade was moving north along and just west of Cemetery Ridge. As the Rebels cleared Daniels' right flank, the cocky Englishman swung his right section out several feet in echelon and faced north, blasting the right of the line.[77]

Just as McGilvery's entire line pummeled the Confederate line, two more veteran units from the artillery park moved over the ridge at top speed and joined the fight. Captain James H. Cooper's 1st Pennsylvania Artillery Battery B of the I Corps Artillery Brigade, with four 3" Ordnance Rifles swung south into McGilvery's line. Only a few days before, Cooper had commanded 114 men, but two days of severe fighting had taken its toll. He was lucky to have four guns as one of his guns had been disabled on July 1st. Moving south along the ridge, Cooper passed Sim's 1st New Jersey Battery B, of the III Corps Artillery Brigade, which was still sitting in reserve on the reverse slope. Most of Sim's men were on the crest watching the fight.

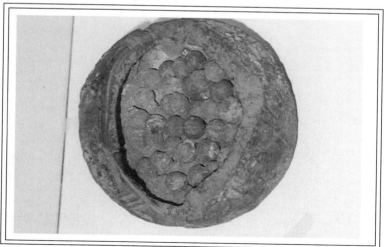

Spherical Case Shot

Swinging around, Cooper's rifles went into position in the gap between Sterling's right flank (2nd Connecticut) and Rank's (the 3rd Pennsylvania) left. (Cooper's position is at the present monument dedicated to the 1st New Jersey Battery B, a unit that did not engage during Picket's Charge.

Cooper came into battery too late to engage the right flank of Pickett's division, but to his front at 800 yards was another column cresting the Emmitsburg Road. Using the Klingle house for distance, 2,400 feet away, Cooper opened with

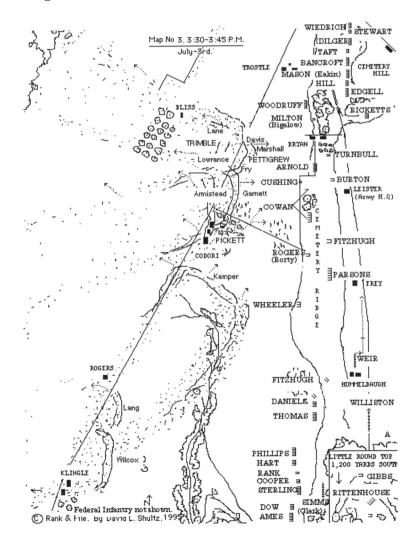

shell on a battery posted near the barn. His first round blew through the barn, exploded inside, and set it on fire. Many Federal wounded from July 2nd would die in the blaze that engulfed the structure.[78]

Following Cooper onto Cemetery Ridge were the remaining three rifles belonging to the 13th New York Independent Battery, commanded by Lieutenant William Wheeler. The 13th continued west over the ridge and reported to Hancock. Hancock personally led Wheeler a few yards north of the Vermont Brigade and pointed toward Rogers' section south of the Copse of Trees. Wheeler swung his guns into a gap just vacated by an infantry regiment as they moved northward following the parade. Within a few seconds, Wheeler opened with canister, blowing away both friend and foe as the heavy smoke concealed identities. The gruesome parade continued north.

Throughout the Confederates' march across the Plum Run valley, McGilvery's line had exploded at almost point-blank range with a destructive enfilade fire. Yet what was left of the Confederate line bravely continued on. In a post-war letter, Captain. Edwin Dow, commanding the 6th Maine Light said it best:

> My Battery was on the left and Pickett was aiming at our center. My guns, and thirty of the other five batteries around me, sent a hail of shot and shell into their right flank. I tell you, the gaps we made were simply terrible. But they closed up their lines, and closed up and closed them up, till they got to within a hundred yards of our line in the center. I tell you, it looked bad from my position when the Confederate line went at ours in the center.[79]

The Angle

South of the Copse of Trees, Hunt stood watching through his binoculars, as Cowan engaged the enemy with positive effect. His rifled guns, along with Fitzhugh's, Burton's and Daniels', tore great gaps in Pickett's line as it crested the first rise in full view. Their firing was at its most effective when a distraction near Cowan caught Hunt's attention. A mounted II Corps aide had entered the battery and was pleading with

Cowan to move to the north. Cowan initially refused, saying that he was assigned to Doubleday's command. At this time, Cowan, Hunt, Doubleday, Newton, and even Weir looked north, and there, in Perrin's (Brown's) vacated battery position near the Copse of Trees, stood Brigadier General Alexander Webb, waving his hat, beckoning for aid.[80]

Not waiting for orders, Cowan gave the command, and the guns were hooked up and pulled out of action into column by pieces. They moved north toward the Copse of Trees at a brisk trot. Although the distance was short, the battery was impeded by hundreds of infantrymen also moving into new positions. Hunt, now mounted, rode a few yards west to Fitzhugh to order more support for Webb.

Pulling up alongside Fitzhugh, Hunt pointed to Cowan's battery, which was moving north. Fitzhugh understood the order, immediately rode to his guns and ordered his left section limbered. Covered by the fire from the center section, the two left rifles pulled out and followed Burton's right section of the 11th New York. Parsons, not to be outdone, flew by Fitzhugh, and followed Cowan to the north. Parsons had pulled out of McGilvery's line without orders after witnessing the goings on. With a limited field of fire to his front due to massed infantry four lines deep, Parsons thought it prudent to move north, a move that would prove itself remarkable in time.

Cowan moved north quickly, his six rifles covering the distance in less than one minute. His cannoneers rode on the chests, several even climbing on to the gun carriages, while holding on to their implements. The young grim-faced artillerymen hung on as their column careened through infantry regiments that were moving up, scattering the swearing soldiers in all directions. Cowan's first gun overran the intended position and moved past the Copse of Trees into the space occupied by Cushing's 4th U. S. Battery A. Cowan's five other pieces swung around at reverse trot and dropped trail on the left of the Copse of Trees. Following Webb's directions into battery, Cowan ordered case in his left five tubes, then rode to the north of the thickets to check on his solitary gun.[81]

Riding into Cushing's position, Cowan couldn't help but notice the demolished battery and its wounded commander. Staying mounted, Cowan approached Cushing, who was bent over clutching his stomach. Despite his severe wounds, the feisty lieutenant was pushing his two serviceable rifles down the ridge to the stone wall. Politely addressing Cushing, Cowan asked the lieutenant, "Is my piece crowding you sir?" Cushing responded by regaining his composure and straightening up. He told Cowan, "Your piece is fine where it's at. I see it causing no problems."[82]

The two officers then returned to their duties. As Cowan turned back toward his single rifle, which sat very near Cushing's disabled left piece just north of the Copse of Trees, he heard Cushing yell "Forward to the wall!"[83] Cushing and his crew stacked their canister next to the two guns by the stone wall, near the Angle and waited for the enemy to close a bit more.

General Hunt arrived on the scene and was approached by Hazard and Captain Bingham, who handed Hunt Meade's written order. Hazard congratulated Hunt for his quick response. Hunt was shocked by the corpse-littered landscape at the remnants of Hazard's II Corps Artillery Brigade. After acknowledging Hazard's congratulations, he asked about the condition of the rest of Hazard's command. Rogers (Rorty), Cushing and Arnold where all cut to pieces and basically unfit for action. Still, they held their positions, not by order, but by their own choice.

Rogers sat waiting, his two 10-pounder Parrotts loaded with canister. He had just finished firing his last two rounds of case at Pickett's lines as they neared the Emmitsburg Road. One of his guns was being served mostly by volunteer infantrymen from the 15th Massachusetts, who threw everything they could get their hands on, including rocks, bayonets, cups, spoons and nails into the tube to fire at the enemy. They waited patiently as their comrades to their left cocked their rifled muskets. Cushing and his remaining men waited behind the wall at the Angle. Arnold's Rhode Islanders sat behind their low wall in rear of Cushing. They had a few case shells still in their chests and were waiting the order to reopen fire. Arnold's gunners wiped the grime from their blackened faces as General Alexander Hays, commanding the troops on Arnold's right, put his entire division through the manual of arms.

From the Bryan orchard, Turnbull continued to fire solid shot over the heads of Cushing's men. Ricketts' missiles from Cemetery Hill flew high over the ridge, exploding with precision among the Rebel lines now cresting a rise between the Emmitsburg Road and the Bliss farm. The Federal skirmish line opened with a resounding roar which was heard back on Cemetery Hill. Hancock rode past his batteries and down to the

Emmitsburg Road, rallying his skirmishers, while Milton still fired his two 12-pounders with spherical case and shot.

Woodruff's gunners fired the last of their solid shot at the attacking lines. From their position in front of Ziegler's Grove, it appeared as if the enemy skirmish-line was going to flank them and carry their position. Then Woodruff's rapid fire of long-range canister, although sending panicked Federal skirmishers diving for cover, helped drive the thin Confederate line back, ending the threat from due west. As previously stated, the main Confederate line to their front was now angling to the southwest and away from Battery I, offering Woodruff's men a fine opportunity to enfilade the entire enemy line.[84]

Woodruff opened as the enemy line began to descend the rise east of the Bliss farm, marching toward the Emmitsburg Road. His guns fired canister, turning the plank fence into kindling and blowing holes twenty to thirty feet wide in the first advancing gray lines. By this time, the gaps on the Confederate left failed to close completely. The line became ragged and broken, but still the Charge continued.

There were numerous fences in this area, and though much of the plank fence along the Emmitsburg Road had been partially dismantled by the fighting on July 2nd, enough was left to make it an impediment to the attacking infantry. Many unlucky Confederates met their death while trying to cross these fences running perpendicular to Woodruff's oblique-facing battery. Their bodies, caught in grotesque postures, dangled from the fences where they died. "Fire at will" was Woodruff's order as the fight became general. Musketry began to take its toll as the Rebels began to fire back in solid volleys.

Milton was now completely engaged. His 12-pounders were helping Woodruff's guns pound the lines to pieces at 300 yards. His 9th Massachusetts was cheered on by men from the infantry regiments as they passed through his two guns. Masked by the Bryan barn, Milton switched back to his few remaining solid shots as the closest enemy line began to disappear from his field of fire.

Arnold was also engaged, sending his last few shells into the exposed lines of the enemy. As the Confederate line approached the plank fence bordering the Emmitsburg Road, it broke into a run, anticipating cover in the somewhat sunken road. Arnold's fire smashed into the planking as the Confederate line attempted to dress its ranks before crossing. Many Rebels were killed in their attempt to scale the fence, and many more were hit while crowding into the openings caused by the fighting on July 2nd. Others lost their nerve at this point and simply fell back from the fence and either lay down or turned back. Yet others continued on, crossed the road and headed up the slope.

Cowan continued to fire case and shrapnel into the Codori Orchard and the Emmitsburg Road. As the Federal skirmish line began to pull back, Rebels began pouring over the road in mass, swarming around Codori's farm and driving Hancock's skirmishers before them.

Parsons had unlimbered on top of the ridge, behind a worm fence, with low stone walls on either flank. The small stone Peter Frey house sat directly east of and behind, along the Taneytown Road. Parsons continued with shrapnel, probably firing to the south of the Codori barn at the advancing lines now in the Emmitsburg Road.

Confederate batteries that had advanced to the Emmitsburg Road, and those posted at the Rogers' house west of it, began to get Parson's range. His first casualty occurred here, only moments after he had opened. One of his German drivers was hit ever so lightly by a piece of shell that had exploded above his head, and, according to Parsons, "He raised up six inches in the saddle and then settled back down, seemingly unhurt. The old German dismounted and stood for a moment, wobbled, then fell dead." As the attackers came up the slope, Battery A switched to timed-fuse shells, cutting the fuses to two seconds, with three degrees elevation, just enough to clear the Federal infantry line to Parson's front.[85]

12 pounder Ball With Sabot

Fitzhugh's section from Battery K opened from the left rear of Cowan, firing timed case over the Federal infantry at the enemy crossing the Emmitsburg Road. Capt. John D. Burton looked for a clear field of fire as he led his section to the right of Fitzhugh, north of the Copse of Trees. Burton placed his guns on top of the ridge due east of Cushing's hard-hit 4th U. S. Battery A, becoming a bit tangled with some of Cushing's wrecked caissons. Burton opened with percussion shell, no doubt firing over the heads of the men of the 72nd Pennsylvania who were posted to his front. Fitzhugh's four rifles switched to timed-fuse shell as the enemy line closed, firing from either side of the thickets and doing good execution.[86]

Passing Rogers' front from left to right at close quarters, perhaps 200 hundred yards away, the right flank of the Rebel line moved up the Emmitsburg Road, trying to align itself. Rogers yelled, "Open fire," and the double blasts of canister spewed forth, blowing the heads off several men caught at the front.[87]   Again, Rogers yelled for double canister, and the Parrotts discharged and recoiled back up the slope, smashing into the enemy. The Johnnies simply lowered their heads and quickened their step to the north, closing to their left as they moved. Federal infantry blasted the lines from around Rogers' position, and the sound was deafening. A man could not even hear his own rifle or pistol discharge in the continuous roll of small arms fire.

With so many men down in Rogers' section, there was no order to the drill. The nearest man, regardless of his rank or assigned duties, picked up the charge and put it in the bore. Whoever had the rammer at the time slammed home the charge, finishing with a ka-thunk. Someone covered the vent, and pricked the powder charge. Then, the person firing the gun inserted the primer into the vent, the lanyard having already been hooked, and the men stepped back and awaited the order to fire. This procedure was being done effectively by Rogers' right gun, which was ably handled by his cannoneers. The left piece, however, was having much more difficulty as three of its principal men were volunteer infantrymen.[88] This also occurred in other batteries.

As the Confederates crossed the Emmitsburg Road and came up the slope, Cushing and Cowan both opened with double canister.   Like others, Cowan felt uncomfortable about the situation and ordered the prolonge ropes to be strung out on the ground behind each gun, just in case they had to withdraw quickly. Some rough ground 500 feet west of the Copse of Trees helped cover the Rebels' advance at this point. Here, for the first time, they stopped and fired their first real effective volley into the faces of the Federal batteries at the Copse of Trees.[89]

Cushing and his first sergeant, Frederick Fuger, continued to order double canister, as the bleeding lieutenant took several more glancing blows from minie balls. Cowan stood at his own right gun, directing fire on the enemy slowly inching forward. The Federal infantry was at its best, standing on its own, firing back at the enemy line.

Lieutenant Turnbull fired spherical case without fuses as he knew the problems with the prematurely exploding 12-pounder case shot. Being a trained regular, Turnbull opted to raise his elevation to three degrees and fire over the heads of his own line, clearing them by several dozen feet. His rounds acted as solid shot, bounding and tearing into the Confederate mob as it moved about the Codori orchard and farm.

Arnold blasted the Confederates caught trying to cross a small plank fence that ran parallel to his gun line 100 yards to his front. The Confederate soldiers on the far left of their line who managed to cross the Emmitsburg Road found this fence their biggest obstacle during their charge. Arnold's infantry support, four lines deep, poured volley after volley into the Confederate ranks from 100 yards away. As on the Confederate right, these lines on the left were forced toward their center. Arnold fed them double canister, blowing huge gaps into the already thinned enemy regiments. Still, they slowly moved forward.

Twenty-four-year-old Lieutenant Tully McCrea, commanding Woodruff's right section, described the attack as it neared Emmitsburg Road:

> When I saw this mass of men approaching our position, and knowing that we had but one thin line of infantry to oppose them, I thought that our chances for kingdom come, or Libby prison were very good. As the enemy started across the field in such splendid array, every rifled battery from Cemetery Hill to Round Top was brought to bear upon their line. We, with the smoothbores, loaded with canister, and bided our time. When arriving within five hundred yards we commenced to fire, and the slaughter

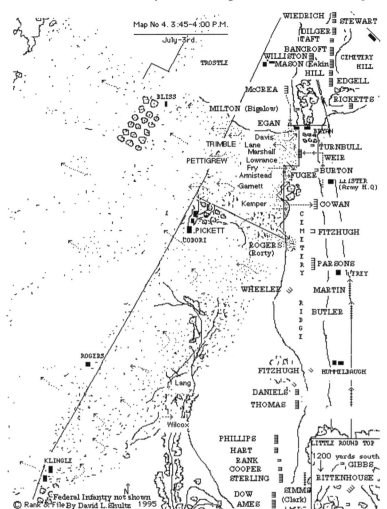

Map No 4. 3:45-4:00 P.M.
July-3rd.

was dreadful. Never was their such a splendid
target for light artillery.[90]

Reinforcements

Five fresh batteries from the VI Corps, as well as
portions of batteries from the XII Corps, moved up in support
of Hancock, Newton and Howard. Back on Cemetery Hill,
Osborn and his batteries poured it on. They never let up for one
moment, not even after most of the attacking columns moved

under the protection of the brow of west Cemetery Hill. Osborn's gunners continued to tear up the earth along the Emmitsburg Road and in the open fields as far east as Seminary Ridge.

Edgell's New Hampshire battery, out of long-range ammunition, was relieved from duty by Osborn, as several VI Corps units passed by along the Taneytown Road. Leading the way from the VI Corps' artillery park was Lt. Edward Williston's 2nd U. S. Artillery Battery D, thought by some to be the finest artillery battery in the Army of the Potomac. They moved past the Cemetery and pulled into battery just west of the road, north of Ziegler's Grove. Williston and his men were held in reserve, facing the Emmitsburg Road several hundred yards northeast of the Emanuel Trostle farm.[91]

Below Williston, Woodruff's gunners fought what they perceived to be a flanking move by the enemy. Masked on the left by the Bryan farm, Woodruff had the uncomfortable feeling that the Rebels had broken through and would attack him from beyond the buildings and orchard. He walked over to his left section, commanded by Lieutenant John Egan, and ordered the lieutenant's two pieces further to the left. As Woodruff turned to walk away he was struck in the body by a minie ball. Egan turned to his commander who told him to get moving. Egan left Woodruff to the care of others, who carried him back into Ziegler's Grove where he leaned up against a tree, bleeding profusely. He died the next day in a II Corps hospital.

Egan mounted his horse and led his section south, a short 70 yards to a stone wall 55 feet north of the Bryan barn. He unlimbered under intense enemy rifle fire, squeezing into a small gap near the Bryan barn. The stone wall to his front still runs west out of Ziegler's Grove, past the Bryan orchard and house, and continues west for 67 feet. Placed by General Hays at the head of the Bryan farm lane behind the stone wall, Egan reopened with double canister to the west-southwest.[92]

Lieutenant Emerson Bicknall of the 1st Massachusetts Sharpshooters barely avoided having his left company destroyed by Egan's fire. His 20-man unit stood engaged in the Bryan farm lane, about 30 yards east of the Emmitsburg Road. Bicknall had seen Egan's two guns being rushed to his left, and, as Egan prepared to fire down the length of the road, Bicknall refused his left flank by pulling it back north of the fence, "giving the two guns at the top of the lane a field of fire, of which they soon cleared."[93] Hays personally directed Egan to fire toward Cushing's wrecked battery as Rebels there began to breach the lines.[94]

Egan's move all but stopped Milton's section's engagement against Pickett's Charge. Milton instead focused on the retreating enemy around the Bliss farm, west of the Emmitsburg Road, as did Lieutenant Tully McCrea, now commanding Woodruff's battery. McCrea had not noticed the absence of Egan's left section, and was extremely relieved when one of his sergeants came through the grove with a wagon-load of ammunition. McCrea reopened with solid shot and case, firing at the mob moving back toward Seminary Ridge.[95]

As Lieutenant Alonzo Cushing yelled "fire!", his two rifles erupted with a deafening roar as their double loads of canister tore into the Rebel ranks. Before either cannon settled back after its recoil, Cushing lunged forward, his lower face shot away. Sergeant Fuger attempted to brake Cushing's fall as the lieutenant crumpled to the ground at his feet, dead. With all the officers from Battery A down, Fuger assumed command. From only 30 yards away, Fuger's two guns blew the enemy line back, and the Rebels wavered for a moment. Then, musketry poured into the battery from the left and right, disabling the left piece. After ordering triple canister to be loaded into the right rifle, Fuger yelled "fire," and the gun exploded, recoiling back three feet. He heard the high-pitched Rebel yell, and a few seconds later, Fuger found himself surrounded and in hand-to-hand combat.[96]

Arnold watched Fuger's fight as he fired double canister on the closing enemy. Seeing Fuger being overrun, Arnold asked for, and received, help from Major John Moore's 99th Pennsylvania infantry. Grabbing hold of Fuger's three disabled pieces on the crest, Maj. Moore and some of his men men hauled them back over the crest out of the enemy's grasp.[97]

Arnold ordered his six guns out by piece, beginning on the right. His first three pieces pulled back without difficulty, leaving the left half-battery to cover their withdrawal. This allowed the Confederates, who were still being pressed to the southeast, to move closer. As two of the left half-battery's guns pulled back, the far-left piece was isolated a few yards to the front. A well directed blast of double canister from this gun felled many men from the South, but not enough. The crew was forced to abandon the gun where it sat, and scamper back east of the ridge. There are many conflicting reports, both Northern and Southern, about this gun possibly being overrun.[98]

Federal infantry swarmed about the Angle area in thick

bunches, trading volley for volley with the thinning Rebel lines still coming over the stone wall and through Cushing's guns.

Lieutenant Gulian Weir, with his 5th U. S. Battery C east of Cowan, had received no orders and was thus unengaged. He began to pull his battery out in column of pieces, heading back to the Artillery Reserve Park. Weir had not even reached the Taneytown Road, 100 yards away, when he was approached by Colonel Warner of Hunt's staff, who yelled, "Weir!, Weir! Every battery is ordered to the front." Having just been on the front where no one had wanted his 12-pounders, Weir asked, "Where shall I go in?" Pointing north up the Taneytown Road, Warner said, "Go right up there, someone will show you where to go in."[99]

Weir, motioning forward, shouted commands over the din. Staying west of the Taneytown Road, Weir cut a path through the fields belonging to Peter Frey and Lydia Leister. Keeping well below the eastern brow of Cemetery Ridge, Weir moved past Meade's vacated headquarters and onto the small farm lane that ran up the ridge. Weir saw a young mounted officer and said, "I was ordered here, where shall I go in?" The man pointed up the ridge and said, "Go in over there, you'll come in on their flank and mow 'em down."[100]

Ordering, "Column Left, Trot," Weir charged his battery by column up east Cemetery Ridge. Cresting the ridge, Weir passed Turnbull, who was posted off his right flank, now secured as the 7th West Virginia infantry double-timed through his section. Weir later wrote: "I saw before me a small open plain, our men on either side. There was to the front several guns lying to the left [Cushing], an open space to my front [Arnold's vacated position], and beyond this gap, a dense body of the enemy."[101]

Weir's first Napoleon was behind him. As he motioned to the right, the lead driver pulled hard, and the gun swung to the right and then back to the left toward the stone wall, circling in reverse to unlimber. At this time, Weir's horse was shot, sending the lieutenant sprawling. Jumping to his feet, Weir looked back and saw that his cannoneers had performed the necessary move to unlimber in front. His battery's position was compact, only fifty yards long at most, barely enough space to work the guns. To his right, Federal infantry had begun to fill the space Arnold had opened, thereby partially closing the gap. They now stood inches away from Weir's right piece. Men from Delaware, Connecticut, New Jersey and New York fought together like demons as the Rebel attack wavered only a few yards away.

Weir's first blast of double canister exploded into the faces of the enemy only twenty feet away. His Napoleons recoiled back from the wall, their wheels crushing over the bodies of dead and wounded artillerymen from Arnold's Rhode Island Battery. Weir's blasts disintegrated the Rebel soldiers to his front. Their crumpled, singed bodies lay on the ground in unidentifiable heaps. The enemy line was stopped in its tracks. The dark-gray mass of men either was blown back or moved to the south, toward the inner wall of the Angle, where many sought shelter and surrendered. The few who kept coming had their hands thrown up in surrender.[102]

South of the Copse of Trees, Capt. Andrew Cowan saw "a Confederate officer not more than 20 feet away. I heard him yell "take that gun," referring to one of my guns. I ordered "fire," and all five blew the line to pieces with double canister. The officer was gone." [103] This would be memorialized after the battle as "Double Canister At Ten Yards." Yet the Confederates kept coming.

Cowan used the prolonge ropes he had previously laid out to begin pulling back. Hunt was now on Cowan's left-front firing his pistol at point-blank range, all the while yelling, "See 'em! See 'em!"[104] As Cowan pulled back to the crest, massed Federal infantry moved up into the position as the enemy infantry dashed over the stone wall. Reopening from the crest, between Fitzhugh and Burton, Cowan fired case with fuses cut at two seconds, with many of the shells exploding prematurely over his own line. Chaos reigned supreme at the Angle.

South of Cowan, Rogers had fought his two Parrotts to the last. One gun had exploded due to the poor handling of the piece by the Massachusetts infantry volunteers. The explosion was so violent that the gun completely flipped over, crushing one man. Two volunteers were dead with five others wounded. Rogers kept up his fight with his right piece firing double and triple canister. A large gap was opened when Federal infantry moved north toward the Copse of Trees. Taking advantage of this, Confederates surged over the wall, aiming for Rogers' section which sat 40 feet east of the wall.[105]

One last blast of double canister cleared his front for a brief moment. Then, the enemy regained its advantage and charged. Corporal Walter Brogan, who fired the last blast of double canister, recalled the scene:

The enemy swept on over all obstacles and around our pieces, and for the first and last time in the history of Battery B, the hands of the foe were laid upon its guns. It was but for a brief moment. Sergeant Darveau fired his revolver at the foe as they came on, and when an officer planted his colors on a gun, exclaiming, "This is our gun", Sergeant Darveau seized the trail hand-spike, and struck him full across the forehead, as I blasted him with my revolver, killing him on the spot. . . Darveau fell instantly, riddled with bullets. Our infantry closed around our position and helped rescue our guns taking many prisoners.[106]

Repulse

Lieutenant Wheeler, who was posted a few hundred yards south of Rogers, later wrote about his battery's fire: "This gave me an opportunity to enfilade their column with canister which threw them into great disorder, and brought them to a halt three times." Wheeler's timing was nearly perfect. His 13th New York helped to beat back the deepest Confederate penetration into the Federal lines during Pickett's Charge.[107]

Help also came from the 151st Pennsylvania, whose move north had brought them to Rogers' battery. Captain Walter Owens of the 151st stated: "We moved following the others, loading and firing as we ran. One gun to our front was seized by the enemy and we poured it to them."[108] What was left of the Rebel line pulled back west of the wall and Rogers' survivors reclaimed their only remaining gun. Many Confederates had thrown themselves down west of the wall to escape Wheeler's doses of double canister and Owens' well-directed volleys. They now asked for quarter as Federal infantry reinforcements arrived on the scene.

Wheeler realigned his guns and continued with canister into Pickett's massed lines. Then two regiments from the Vermont Brigade, posted to Wheeler's left, counter-charged up Plum Run, forcing Wheeler to cease fire when the line of blue infantry crossed into his field of fire. He realigned his three rifles and concentrated on an enemy battery that was engaging from the Emmitsburg Road, just south of the Codori barn.

All along Cemetery Ridge, the shot-torn enemy turned and retreated back down the slope toward the Emmitsburg Road. Hancock's thin line had held. The Federal artillery massed on top of the ridge east of the Copse of Trees continued to fire assorted projectiles at the retreating Confederates. From Cemetery Hill south to Cowan at the Angle, they all played on the enemy infantry, paying little mind to the Rebel batteries now posted along the Emmitsburg Road. Cowan ordered his right section back to the stone wall to his previous position left of the Copse of Trees, and reopened with canister at the retreating enemy. The two rifles switched to shell as they re-targeted against a Confederate battery in the road.

Yet now a second Confederate line appeared, headed toward Cemetery Ridge. Two brigades led by Brigadier General Cadmus Wilcox and Colonel David Lang stepped off some 20 minutes after the main Charge.

On Little Round Top, Rittenhouse had no way of knowing what was happening. He saw the new Confederate line across the Emmitsburg Road and began firing on them. Unlike the first line, this one did not oblique to the left and move north, up the Emmitsburg Road, but chose to attack due east. As Private George Clark in Wilcox's ranks wrote, "Pickett's division for some reason moved away from the attack and disappeared from my view." The enemy line lay posted ahead as the Alabama Brigade attacked it alone.[109]

The Federal cannons now concentrated on the small gray line included, from left to right starting on Little Round Top: Rittenhouse with four, Ames with six, Dow with four, Sterling with six, Cooper with four, Rank with two, Hart with four, Phillips with six, Thomas with six, Daniels with six, Fitzhugh's center section with two, and Wheeler with three. Parsons fired into Lang but mainly concentrated on counter battery fire along the Emmitsburg Road. Altogether, 59 cannons blasted this line before it cleared the Emmitsburg Road. Its attack, in essence, was already over.[110]

Rittenhouse persisted without letting up, sending shell and case from perfect right enfilade. As they moved east toward Plum Run, the Confederates were torn into small bunches. This time the gaps did not close. One part of the line stopped at a worm fence to the right of the hillock (south) along Plum Run. Its right was all but obliterated as McGilvery's left flank batteries blew the fence line into kindling.[111]

The Federal gunners on McGilvery's left cheered as the

right half retreated in mass disorder back over the Emmitsburg Road, leaving 300 more casualties scattered about the fields. As Federal infantry advanced to take charge of prisoners and mop up, they passed through McGilvery's left flank, ending the action of the batteries posted there. Three hundred yards to the north, Lang was still being punished. Daniels, upset that his Michigan battery's field of fire was obscured by the 13th and 16th Vermont as they moved north, ordered his right section to face about and rejoined the other four guns in a perfectly executed enfilade on the second Confederate line's left flank. By the scores, soldiers from the main attack force also moved back through the second line, making its advance that much more difficult.

Fitzhugh's center section, along with Daniels', Thomas's, Phillip's and Hart's guns unloaded case and shell, then canister, into the new line. Approaching Plum Run thickets, Lang looked about and saw no support. For the first time, he saw McGilvery's entire right flank artillery line. He realized that "to continue forward would be murder," and he ordered his line back, "all men for themselves." Somehow the left regiment did not get the message and continued on.[112] Stopping just west of Plum Run, they tried to form a firing line. One well-directed volley of double canister from Thomas's Napoleons devoured the color guard of a Confederate regiment. Thomas watched the flag fall to the ground, only to see it raised minutes later by a soldier in blue.[113] Daniels ordered a cease fire too late and the last volley of his canister caught men from the 14th Vermont, who were moving rapidly forward toward the Rebels.[114] Several volleys from the thinned enemy ranks felled Vermonters in rapid fashion. All of the 29 killed from the 14th Vermont died from wounds received on July 3rd, mostly during this charge, although how many were injured from the cannonade and how many by Daniels' and Thomas's last blasts of canister will never be known.

The repulse of the second Confederate wave ended the threat to the Federal center. Most of McGilvery's line returned to counter-battery fire while Federal infantry moved past Thomas and through Daniels, collecting prisoners and establishing a strong skirmish line along Plum Run. Fitzhugh's center section limbered to the north to rejoin the rest of the battery as Confederate shells continued to slam onto the ridge.

More Reinforcements

After watching the fight from atop south Cemetery Ridge, Sims led the 1st New Jersey Battery B into McGilvery's line. He squeezed in somewhere to the right of Cooper, too late to engage the retreating enemy. Some units from the VI Corps moved up the Taneytown Road. The 5th U. S. Battery F pulled into Ziegler's Grove, followed by the 2nd U. S. Battery G. Battery F, commanded by Lieutenant Leonard Martin, swung its six 10-pounder Parrotts into battery to the north of McCrea (Woodruff), about 40 yards to his right and rear. Lieutenant John Butler, commanding Battery G, put his six 12-pounders into line on Martin's right. Both Martin and Butler engaged the last of Lee's retreating troops, firing case and shell into the McMillan Woods along Seminary Ridge. Their fire was halted, and they were told to prepare for another attack.

From Weir, posted at the inner Angle, north to Williston on the Taneytown Road, Hunt's line consisted of 28 12-pounder Napoleons and six Parrott rifles, a total of 34 guns covering north Cemetery Ridge. This was quite a formidable line, much stronger than before the attack. Together with Osborn's batteries on Cemetery Hill and the six 12-pounder of McCartney's 1st Massachusetts, 77 guns protecting that area. All were now being supplied with sufficient ammunition to meet another attack.

McCartney had moved his battery up the Taneytown Road following Butler. He pulled off to the right into the Cemetery occupying Hall's and Norton's vacated positions near the little knoll and the small woods. McCartney opened with his six Napoleons, firing at the retreating Confederates along Seminary ridge. After four rounds, he secured his pieces because he could not see the results of his fire.

Three more batteries from Colonel Charles Tompkins VI Corps Artillery Brigade moved in column up the Taneytown Road. Leading the group was the 1st Rhode Island Light Battery G, commanded by Captain George Adams. Moving past McCartney, Adams stopped his six rifles in rear of Ziegler's Grove, south of Williston, keeping in column. Captain Richard Waterman's 1st Rhode Island Light Battery C, with six 12-pounder Napoleons pulled up behind Adams in rear of Ziegler's Grove, keeping in column.

Trailing Adams and Waterman came the 3rd New York Independent Battery, commanded by Lieutenant William Harn.

This battery was the last of the seven VI Corps batteries at Gettysburg. Harn's six 10-pounder Parrotts moved up the Taneytown Road following Waterman, but never made it to Cemetery Hill. Commandeered by one of Hancock's staff, the battery was led past the Leister house to the foot of the small farm lane. Here, the aide pointed west up the ridge directing Harn to where Weir's 5th U. S. had moments earlier moved over the crest.

Harn motioned left and his guns began to ascend east Cemetery Ridge, just north of the Leister House. As his front limber moved off the road, a large mass of Confederates came pouring over the crest. "Get your guns out of here or you'll lose them for sure," yelled the excited aide as he galloped off in another direction to avoid capture. Harn swung around to the right and recrossed the Taneytown Road. He unlimbered east of the road and prepared to open on the closing enemy from no more than 100 yards away. He was lucky. Harn finally realized that the men were prisoners and simply secured his position for the remainder of the battle. He sustained no casualties, nor did he fire a single round. Adding these three batteries to the others on this line, there were 95 guns ready for action.[115]

Captain Hazard mounted a horse and began to inspect his command. Riding to the right past Burton, he found Arnold in rear of the ridge. He ordered Arnold to consolidate with Cushing's serviceable guns for the remainder of the afternoon and prepare for action. Cowan was in the Copse of Trees securing his lone rifle that had been temporarily abandoned by its crew. It was removed to the left and placed with the two guns at the wall, which were already secured. His other half-battery on top the ridge, along with Parsons' and Fitzhugh's full batteries, continued counter-battery fire with percussion shell at the enemy guns in the Emmitsburg Road, doing excellent execution and driving the enemy gunners back from their batteries.

Portions of two XII Corps batteries unlimbered left of Parsons on top of Cemetery Ridge. One was Lieutenant Sylvanus T. Rugg's 4th U. S. Battery H, with four 12-pounder Napoleons. This battery had been hit hard during the cannonade as it sat below and south of Cemetery Hill, just west of the Baltimore Pike. On reaching Cemetery Ridge, Rugg opened on the retreating Confederates with spherical case as the enemy moved back toward the woods along Seminary Ridge. The other battery was Lieutenant William Van Reed's section of 12-

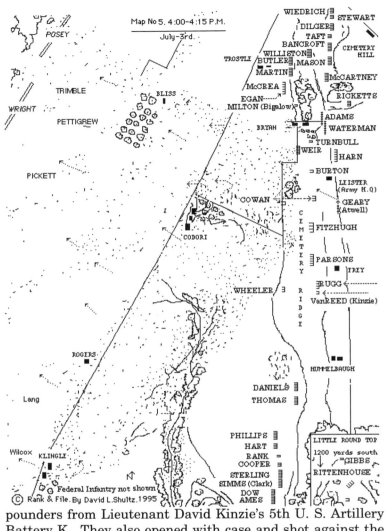

pounders from Lieutenant David Kinzie's 5th U. S. Artillery
Battery K. They also opened with case and shot against the
retreating infantry and the batteries along the Emmitsburg
Road.[116]

Victory

With Pickett's Charge routed, Gillette's reserve
ammunition wagons began to rumble onto the ridge to resupply
the forward batteries. Most of the batteries remained where

they had engaged, preparing for another enemy attack. Confederate artillery continued sporadic fire in attempts to cover the retreat as the Federal gunners still zeroed in on the few retreating men who scampered across the undulating fields.

On Cemetery Hill Osborn's gunners continued to hammer the retreating Rebels relentlessly, switching to counter-battery fire only after ordered to do so by General Howard.

Hazard's and McGilvery's guns engaged enemy batteries posted well west of the Emmitsburg Road in the Peach Orchard and Pitzer and McMillan Woods, forcing many Confederate batteries back under cover. One Rebel battery that moved into position northeast of the burning Klingle barn was destroyed from the concentrated fire from at least eight Federal batteries. Ames, Sterling, Cooper, Hart, Phillips, Thomas, Daniels, Wheeler, and Parsons all mentioned in their post battle reports that their fire destroyed one enemy battery posted near the burning barn. If this one poor battery was the victim of all their reports, it explains why all of its gunners left their wrecked battery and scampered back over the Emmitsburg Road. The Rebel gunners were allowed to return, unmolested, a few hours later and pull their wrecked guns back over the road as the Federals looked on.

As Pickett's men withdrew, General Alexander Hays, commander of the II Corps division just north of the Angle, had ridden up to Lieutenant Egan's section of Woodruff's battery, still sitting near the Bryan barn. Egan's smoking 12-pounders were secured as cheering infantry moved over the wall, taking prisoners. General Hays spurred his horse forward, jumped over the wall into the lane and continued past the splintered plank fence into the field beyond. Grabbing a Confederate battle flag that dangled from a small tree directly in front of Egan, Hays proceeded south in front of his 3rd Division line toward Fuger's (Cushing's) wrecked battery at the Angle, dragging the Rebel flag in the dirt behind him as he rode.[117]

General Meade, accompanied by his son, rode onto the ridge up a small path leading to the Bryan house from the Taneytown Road. Moving west over the ridge, Meade rode up to Lt. Egan and asked, "Where is General Hays?" Egan pointed to the south and watched Meade as the general surveyed the area for a few moments. Meade then asked, "Have they turned?" The lieutenant responded by answering, "Yes, sir! See there, General Hays has one of their flags." Meade shot back, "I don't care about their flags, have they turned?" Egan then reported, "Yes sir, they are just turning."[118]

Lieutenant Gulian Weir secured his six Napoleons at the inner Angle and took stock of the situation. He cleared the prisoners from his front, telling them as he pointed east, "Go down that way, you will be taken care of. I wish I could go with you." Weir recalled that hundreds of wounded lay about the battery during the attack. He wrote, "I remembered the distinct sound of enemy bullets striking the wounded and dead that laid about me." His battery's only fatality that day was his horse. One sergeant did have his leg blown off, but he survived the amputation. Weir continued,

> I walked to the left to see General Webb who, I think, was slightly wounded and was resting close to and rear of his lines [under the Copse of Trees]. On Webb's orders I held my position until I was assured that there would not be another attack.[119]

Aftermath

After the war, Capt. James Johnson of the 5th Florida wrote about what he witnessed from within the swale just west of the Emmitsburg Road:

> As Pickett's lines approached and passed over us going to the front, a man plopped down next to me. I thought he was killed or wounded. He said 'No sir, but I can't go forward.' I gave him a slight punch with my sword and told him to go to the rear. I pointed him the way and he unbuckled his cartridge belt; leaving that and his musket, he started. And I thought it would take a pretty swift bullet to overtake him.[120]

This eyewitness account tells of how not one, but many, of Lee's men must have felt as they neared the Emmitsburg Road, facing almost certain death.

To defeat one's enemy, one must neutralize his offensive power. This does not necessarily mean one has to kill the enemy. To immobilize and demoralize him often works just as well. The Federal artillery during Pickett's Charge did just that.

There will never be an accurate count of all the men killed and wounded while serving the batteries during Pickett's Charge. Many of the gunners had been detailed from nearby infantry units, and, unless they had been officially detached, their deaths were simply recorded on the casualty list from their respective regiments as killed in action on July 3rd. Not including the cannonade, at least 13 artillerymen were listed as officially killed during Pickett's Charge.[121] The total was surely higher.

Lieutenant Homer Baldwin of Weir's 5th U. S. Battery C wrote home to his father on July 7, 1863, explaining the batteries' action at the Angle:

> I never saw such a battlefield. On the 3rd every recoil of our guns would send them over the dead and wounded, and flashes of our pieces would scorch and set fire to the clothing of those that lay in front of us. I have seen many a big battle, most of the big ones of this war, and I never saw the likes as this one. It was a glorious victory.[122]

Young Baldwin went on to explain that he had taken a sword from a Confederate captain and was sending it home. He also assumed command of Battery C as Weir was hospitalized for minor wounds and a sore throat.

Captain John Burton of the 11th New York Independent Battery, which was posted to the left rear of Weir, remembered that, after the fighting had stopped, "I walked a short distance to the right of our guns to look over the ground. Scarcely a square yard of this immense field in front of us but was covered with either dead or wounded." The captain spied a Confederate soldier, who was laying against one of the stone walls and beckoning to him for aid. As Burton approached the wounded soldier, the man asked the captain if he would relay a message to his mother. Burton handed him a pencil and an envelope, and the soldier wrote: "Tell my mother I died trusting in the Lord." He then signed the message "John T. Burton, 38th Virginia Infantry." Capt. Burton assured the soldier that the message would be relayed to his mother and that he hoped his wounds would not prove fatal. Capt. Burton also let the dying soldier know that their names where the same. Burton was true to his word, sending the message through the lines at White Plains, Virginia, a few weeks later after his battery had crossed the Potomac River.[123]

Lieutenant Richard Milton, commanding the two Napoleons of the 9th Massachusetts Light, and a few of his men including cannoneer Levi Baker left their battery's position and walked to the left toward the Copse of Trees. Baker later wrote about what he saw: "I recognized then and there that this battle was to be, in all probability regarded as the great turning point in history . . . The ridge where Cushing went down beside his guns, where hand to hand conflict took place, is regarded as the high water mark of the rebellion."[124] With Pickett's Charge repulsed, Lee pulled back to a defensive position west of Gettysburg while Hunt secured his batteries. With the exception of a few minor skirmishes, the Battle of Gettysburg was over.

On July 3rd, 1863, Brigadier General Henry Jackson Hunt, Chief of Artillery, Army of the Potomac, made efficient and effective use of the full power of the resources at his disposal. Of the approximately 12,000 Confederate infantrymen that began the assault known as Pickett's Charge, one-third or fewer made it to the Federal lines. Most attacking Confederates were repulsed well short of their goal. At the beginning of the attack, 111 Federal cannons fired from positions at enfilade, and front defilade, a perfect crossfire that Lee's attacking legions had to move through for nearly one mile. A line of dead and wounded Southerners stretching all the way back to Seminary Ridge testified to the success of the Federal artillery. By the time the Charge was repulsed, 134 guns were engaged. Within minutes after the repulse, there were 158 cannons facing Seminary Ridge. During the Charge and repulse a total of 163 cannons from 36 batteries had engaged and helped repulse the most famous infantry attack in American history.

Footnotes

[1] The rank of each individual given here is the functional rank held at the moment. Captain Andrew Cowan, for example, held a commission as a Lieutenant, but was breveted captain. He had been given an informal promotion but was still on the official roles as a Lieutenant and paid at that rank, but functioned as a captain. Also, the number of guns given for a command is the number actually in use at the moment. For example, Lieutenant Alonzo Cushing began the battle with six guns, but during the Charge had only two. Also, the officer currently in charge

is given as the unit commander, with the previous commander's name in parentheses in the first citation. For example, the 9th Massachusetts Light Artillery, Battery I, had fought fiercely on July 2nd under the command of Captain John Bigelow, who had been wounded. It was commanded on July 3rd by Lt. Richard Milton, and will thus be cited as Milton's 9th Massachusetts (Bigelow).

[2] Report of Henry Jackson Hunt, *The War of the Rebellion: Official Records of the Union and Confederate Armies* (Washington, D.C.: United States Government Printing Office, 1880-1900), 237. All citations are from Vol. XXVII, parts I and II, unless otherwise noted. Hereafter cited as *OR*, I, 237.

[3] Hunt to Bachelder, January 20, 1873, *The Bachelder Papers: Gettysburg in Their Own Words* Volume I Edited By David L. and Audrey J. Ladd (Dayton: Morningside House, 1994), 428-429. Hereafter cited as *Bachelder Papers*.

[4] E. P. Alexander, *The Personal Recollections of Edward Porter Alexander* Edited by Gary Gallagher (Chapel Hill: The University of North Carolina Press, 1989), 245.

[5] Doubleday, *OR*, I, 259, and James, *OR*, I, 591.

[6] Captain Irish, McGilvery's aide, went to the artillery park. Who he reported to or asked for reinforcements is unknown. See McGilvery's report, *OR*, I, 884.

[7] Report of Capt. Patrick Hart, *OR*, I, 888.

[8] Report of Lt. Richard S. Milton. *OR*, I,886; Richard Milton to Mother, July 4, 1863, 9th Massachusetts Infantry file, Gettysburg National Military Park Archives, (hereafter referred to as GNMP).

[9] Capt. Charles A. Phillips to Maj. McGilvery, July 6, 1863, GNMP.

[10] John W. Busey, *These Honored Dead: The Union Casualties at Gettysburg* (Hightstown, N.J.: Longstreet House, 1988), 245.

[11] Frederick Fuger, "Battle of Gettysburg and Personal Recollections of the Battle," 21, Alexander Webb Papers, Yale University. Photocopy in GNMP.

[12] Hunt to Sherman, February, 1882, *Bachelder Papers*, II, 815.

[13] Report of Brig. Gen. Robert O. Tyler, *OR*, I, 872.

[14] Sheldon to Pettit, July 5, 1863, GNMP.

[15] Maj. Gen. John Newton, *OR*, I, 262.

[16] McGilvery's report, *OR*, I, 883-4.

[17] O. W. Damon, "War Diary of O. W. Damon," July 3, 1863, GNMP.

[18] Lieut. Cornelius Gillette, *OR*, I, 878.

[19] Hunt to Bachelder, July 27,1888, *Bachelder Papers*, I, 675. Edward B. Longacre, *The Man Behind The Guns: A Biography of Henry*

J. Hunt, Commander of Artillery,. Army of the Potomac (New York: A. S. Barnes & Co., 1977), 161. L. Van Loan Naisawald, *Grape and Canister* (New York: Oxford University Press, 1960), 365.

[20] Hunt to Bachelder, July 27, 1880, *Bachelder Papers*, I, 675.

[21] *Ibid.*

[22] Henry J. Hunt, "The Third Day At Gettysburg," in *Battle and Leaders of the Civil War: The Tide Shifts.* Volume III (New York: Century Co., 1889), 371-372.

[23] Hunt, *OR*, I, 237.

[24] *Official Records and History of the 1st Michigan Light Artillery in the Civil War* (Kalamazoo: Ihling Brothers & Everard, 1909), 175-190.

[25] Weir to Bachelder, August, 1885, GNMP, quoted in Richard Rollins, ed., *Pickett's Charge: Eyewitness Accounts* (Redondo Beach, CA: Rank and File Publications, 1994), 301.

[26] Report of Lieut. Richard Milton, *OR*, I, 886.

[27] Hunt, *OR*, I, 239; Tyler, 874; Gillette, 878-879; Capt. James Robertson, 1021; Michael Hanifen, *History of Battery B, 1st New Jersey Artillery* (New York: Neale, 1905), 81.

[28] Hunt, *OR*, I, 239.

[29] Hanifen, *History of Battery B*, 81; Capt. Judson Clark, *OR*, I, 586.

[30] Alexander, *Fighting For The Confederacy*, 251; Brig Gen. Cadmus Wilcox, *OR*, I, 619-620.

[31] See Rollins, ed., *Pickett's Charge*, 136, 153, 157, 163, 164.

[32] Gulian Weir to Bachelder, August, 1885, in Rollins, ed., *Pickett's Charge*, 301; Lieut. Homer Baldwin to Father, July 7, 1863. GNMP.

[33] Fuger, "Battle of Gettysburg," 22.

[34] Freeman Cleaves, *Meade Of Gettysburg* (Norman: University of Oklahoma Press, 1960), 160.

[35] Maj. Thomas W. Osborn, *The Eleventh Corps Artillery At Gettysburg: The Papers of Maj. Thomas W Osborn* ed. Herb S. Crumb (Hamilton, N.Y.: Edmonston Publishing, 1990), 37, 72-73.

[36] *Ibid.*

[37] *Ibid.*

[38] Report of Maj. Gen. Oliver O. Howard, *OR*, I, 706.

[39] Osborn, *Eleventh Corps*, 39.

[40] Hart to Hunt, June 30, 1879, *Bachelder Papers*, I, 827.

[41] Report of Capt. Charles Phillips, *OR*, I, 885; Report of Capt. Patrick Hart, *OR*, I, 888; Hunt to Bachelder, January 6, 1866, *Bachelder Papers*, I, 229-304-5.

[42] Report of Lt. Col. McGilvery, *OR*, I, 884.

[43] Osborn, *Eleventh Corps*, 39.

[44] *Ibid.*, 75-76.

[45] *Ibid.*; Hunt to Bachelder, January 20, 1873, *Bachelder Papers,* I, 430.

[46] Capt. James Huntington to Bachelder, June 6, 1878, *Bachelder Papers*, I, 622.

[47] Report of Capt. Frederick M. Edgell, *OR,* I, *892-893.*

[48] Report of Capt. Elijah Taft, *OR,* I, 891-892.

[49] Osborn, *Eleventh Corps,* 70-72. Today's present monument to Taft's section inside the Cemetery does not mark the position of the three replacement guns. It would have been physically impossible to fire down the Emmitsburg Road from the position of today's monument.

[50] Capt. James Stewart, *Compiled History of the Sixth Field Artillery, 1798-1932* (Harrisburg, PA: Telegraph Press, 1933), 54-55.

[51] Hunt to Bachelder, January 6, 1866, *Bachelder Papers,* I, 229.

[52] Bingham to Hancock, January 5, 1869, *Ibid.,* 353.

[53] John Rhodes, *History of Battery B First Rhode Island Light Artillery in the War to Preserve the Union* (Providence: Snow and Farnham, 1884), 204-205.

[54] *Ibid.*

[55] Cowan, *Bachelder Papers,* I, 281, and *OR,* I, 690; *Grape and Canister,* 415-416.

[56] Hunt to Bachelder, January 20th, 1873, *Bachelder Papers,* I, 432.

[57] Hunt to Bachelder, August 22, 1874, *Bachelder Papers,* I, 441.

[58] Lt. Col. John S. Hammell to Bachelder, undated, *Ibid.,* 423.

[59] Fitzhugh, *OR,* I, 896.

[60] Lt. Col. Norbonne Berkeley, undated letter, GNMP.

[61] Osborn, *11th Corp Artillery,* 40, 76-78.

[62] Hunt to Bachelder, August 22, 1875, *Bachelder Papers,* I, 439.

[63] Capt. John Hazard, *OR,* I, 480.

[64] Osborn, *11th Corps Artillery,* 79.

[65] *Ibid.,* 37-38; Lieut. James McCartney, *OR,* I, 688-689. McCartney mistakes Edgell's New Hampshire battery for Norton's Ohio Light.

[66] Report of Ricketts, *Ibid.,* 894; Allan Nevins, *A Diary of Battle: The Personal Journals of Col. Charles S. Wainwright, 1861-1865* (Gettysburg: Stan Clark Military Books, 1962), 249.

[67] Taft, undated letter, GNMP.

[68] Stewart, *Sixth U. S.,* 55.

[69] Report of Brig. Gen. Joseph Davis, *OR,* II, 651.

[70] Maj. McLeod Turner to the *Raleigh Observer,* October 10, 1877,

quoted in Rollins, ed., *Pickett's Charge*, 242.

[71] Osborn, *Philadelphia Weekly Times,* May 10, 1879.

[72] Edgell's report, *OR*, I, 893.

[73] Isaac Trimble, quoted in Rollins, ed., *Pickett's Charge*, 233.

[74] Report of McGilvery, *OR*, I, 884; see also Phillips, 885, Hart, 888, McMahon, 889, Dow, 898, and Ames, 901.

[75] Thomas to Father, July 10, 1863, GNMP.

[76] See the following reports in *OR*, I: Newton, 262; Col. Hiram Berdan, 515; Lt. Col. Casper Tripp, 518; Lt. Col. Charles Merrill, 522; Col. George Burling, 571; Lt. Col. S. R. Gilkyson, 578; Col. Alan Nelson, 497; Maj. John Danks, 498; Col. Calvin Craig, 500, and many others.

[77] Capt. Walter Owens to Col. G. F. McFarland, August 6, 1866, *Bachelder Papers*, I, 269.

[78] Report of Capt. James Cooper, *OR*, I, 365.

[79] Edwin Dow, undated letter, GNMP.

[80] Cowan to Bachelder, August 26, 1866, *Bachelder Papers*, I, 281; Hunt to Bachelder, August 22, 1874, *Ibid.*, 441.

[81] Cowan, *OR*, I, 690; Cowan to Bachelder, August 26, 1866, *Bachelder Papers*, I, 281-282; see also Hunt to Bachelder, August 22, 1874, *Ibid.*, 441.

[82] Cowan to Bachelder, December 2, 1885, *Ibid.*, II, 1157.

[83] *Ibid.*

[84] Tully McCrea, "Reminiscences About Gettysburg," March 30,1904, 5-6, GNMP.

[85] Lt. Augustin Parsons, June 2, 1889, quoted in Rollins, ed., *Pickett's Charge*, 299-300.

[86] Cowan to Bachelder, August 21, 1866, *Bachelder Papers,* I, 281; see also Hazard, *OR*, I, 477-481, and Rollins, ed., *Pickett's Charge*, 290-291, 296, 298.

[87] W. O Beauchamp, "The First New York at Gettysburg," in New York Monument Commission, *New York at Gettysburg, Final Report on the Battlefield of Gettysburg* (Albany: J. B. Lyons and Company, 1902), 1184.

[88] Manuscript "History of the 1st New York Battery B," Orange County Historical Association Syracuse N.Y. Photocopy in GNMP.

[89] Fuger, "Personal Recollections," 22-24; Cowan to Bachelder, August 26,1866, *Bachelder Papers*, I, 282, and Burton to Bachelder, *Ibid.*, 283.

[90] Tully McCrea, "Reminiscences of Gettysburg," March 30, 1864, in Rollins, ed., *Pickett's Charge,* 271.

[91] The present day position would be north of Visitor Center on the Taneytown Road above the parking lot.

[92] H. C. Barrows, "Historical Account," *History of the First Regiment of Artillery*, ed. William Haskin, (Portland, ME: N.P., 1879), 169-170.

[93] Lt. Emerson Bicknall, no date, 1883, GNMP; Capt. Samuel Armstrong to Bachelder, February 6,1884, *Bachelder Papers*, I, 1001.

[94] *History of the First Regiment, U.S. Artillery*, 169.

[95] *Ibid.*, 170.

[96] Fuger, "Battle of Gettysburg," 24.

[97] Rhodes, *History of Battery B*, 217, 219.

[98] *Ibid.*

[99] Gulian Weir, "Recollection of the Third Day At Gettysburg With Battery C," quoted in Rollins, ed., *Pickett's Charge*, 301-302.

[100] *Ibid.*

[101] *Ibid.*

[102] *Ibid.*

[103] Cowan to Bachelder, August 26,1866, *Bachelder Papers*, I, 282.

[104] *Ibid.*, 283.

[105] New York Monument Commission, *New York at Gettysburg*, V. III, 1183-84; Major Samuel Curtis, *OR*, I, 447.

[106] Walter Bogan, "Historical Account, Read by the Reverend W. O. Beauchamp at the Monument Dedication, July 3rd, 1888," GNMP. See also" Manuscript "History of the 1st New York Battery B."

[107] Report of Lt. William Wheeler, *OR*, I, 753

[108] Capt. Walter Owens to Bachelder, August 6, 1866, *Batchelder Papers*, I, 269.

[109] George Clark, quoted in Rollins, ed., *Pickett's Charge*, 184.

[110] See all the post-action reports in the *OR*.

[111] Reports of Capt. Charles Phillips and Capt. Patrick Hart, *OR*, I, 885-888

[112] Capt. James Johnson, quoted in Rollins, ed., *Pickett's Charge*, 164-165; Col. David Lang, *OR*, II, 632-633.

[113] Thomas to Father, July 10, 1863, GNMP.

[114] *Official Records of the First Michigan Light Artillery*, 175-190.

[115] Col. Charles Tompkins to Bachelder, May 24,1875, *Bachelder Papers*, I, 445.

[116] In the area just east of the present day 13th Vermont monument. See Rugg to Bachelder, (no date), 1870, GNMP, and Edmund J. Raus, Jr., *A Generation on the March—The Union Army at Gettysburg* (Lynchburg, VA: H.E. Howard, 1987), 165. and Hancock, *OR*, I, 375.

[117] Unknown newspaper correspondent, quoted in Rollins, ed.,

Pickett's Charge, 262.

[118] Lt. John Egan to Capt. George Meade. Jr, February 8,1870, *Bachelder Papers*, I, 389-390; Capt. George Meade, Jr.., to Bachelder, May 6,1882, *Ibid.*, 852-858.

[119] Weir to Batchelder, quoted in Rollins, ed., *Pickett's Charge*, 302.

[120] Capt. James Johnson, quoted in *Ibid.*, 165.

[121] Busey, *These Honored Dead, passim.*

[122] Lt. Homer Baldwin to Father, July 7,1863, GNMP.

[123] Burton, "Address at Monument Dedication, July 3, 1893," quoted in *New York At Gettysburg*, III, 1308-1309.

[124] Levi Baker, quoted in Rollins, ed., *Pickett's Charge*, xv.

Note: This Order Of Battle contains only those batteries engaged in the repulse of Pickett's Charge, and the number of guns they fired. Several of the batteries mentioned in the text took part in the cannonade but did not fire against the infantry. They are omitted. Other batteries had guns that did not fire at the infantry. The total number of guns on hand will be given in parentheses. The commander at the time of Pickett's Charge is listed. If the battery had more than one commander, they are listed in order.

Order Of Battle Of Batteries Engaged In The Repulse of Pickett's Charge.
Chief of Artillery: Brigadier General Henry Jackson Hunt

I Corps Artillery Brigade. Colonel Charles S. Wainwright.
4th United States Artillery, Battery B. Three 12-pdr. Napoleons. Lt. James Stewart.(6)
1st Pennsylvania Light, Battery B. Four 3-inch Ordnance Rifles. Capt. James H. Cooper.

II Corps Artillery Brigade. Capt. John G. Hazard.
1st New York Artillery, Battery B. Two 10-pdr. Parrott Rifles. Capt. James Rorty. Lt. Albert Sheldon. Lt. Robert E. Rogers.(4)
1st Rhode Island Light, Battery A. Six 3-inch Ordnance Rifles. Capt. William A. Arnold.
1st U. S. Artillery, Battery I. Six 12-pdr. Napoleons. Lt. George A. Woodruff, Lt. Tully McCrea.
4th United States Artillery, Battery A. Two 3-inch Ordnance Rifles. Lt. Alonzo H. Cushing. Lt. Joseph Milne. Sgt. Frederick Fuger.(6)

V Corps Artillery Brigade. Capt. Augustus P. Martin.
5th United States Artillery, Battery D. Six 10-pdr. Parrott Rifles. Lt. Benjamin F. Rittenhouse.

VI Corps Artillery Brigade. Colonel Charles H. Tompkins.

1st Massachusetts Light,Battery A. Six 12-pdr. Napoleons. Capt. William H. McCartney.

New York Light, 1st Battery. Six 3-inch Ordnance Rifles. Capt. Andrew Cowan.

5th U.S.Artillery, Battery F. Six 10-pdr. Parrott Rifles. Lt. Leonard Martin.

2nd U.S. Artillery, Battery G. Six 12-pdr. Napoleons. Lt. John H. Butler.

XI Corps Artillery Brigade. Major Thomas W. Osborn.
1st New York Light, Battery I. Four 3-inch Ordnance Rifles. Capt. Michael Wiedrich.(6)

13th New York Independent Battery. Three 3-inch Ordnance Rifles. Lt. William Wheeler.(4)

1st Ohio Light, Battery, I. Five 12-pdr. Napoleons. Capt. Hubert Dilger.(6)

4th United States Artillery, Battery G. Six 12-pdr. Napoleons. Lt. Eugene A. Bancroft.

XII Corps Artillery Brigade. Lt. Edward D.Muhlenberg.
4th United States Artillery, Battery F. Four 12-pdr Napoleons.Lt. Sylvanus T. Rugg(6).

5th United States Artillery, Battery K. Two 12-pdr Napoleons. Lt. David H. Kinzie.(4)

Artillery Reserve. Brigadier General Robert O. Tyler.

First Regular Brigade. Capt. Dunbar R. Ransom.
1st United States Artillery, Battery H. Six 12-pdr. Napoleons. Lt. Phillip D. Mason.

3rd United States Artillery, Batteries F & K. Two 12-pdr. Napoleons. Lt. John G. Turnbull.(6)

4th United States artillery, Battery C. Six 12-pdr. Napoleons. Lt. Evan Thomas.

5th United States Artillery, Battery C. Six 12-pdr Napoleons. Lt. Gulian V. Weir.

First Volunteer Brigade. Lt. Colonel Freeman McGilvery.
5th Massachusetts Light Artillery, Battery E. Three 3-inch Ordnance Rifles. Capt. Charles Phillips.

9th Massachusetts Light Artillery. Two 12-pdr. Napoleons. Lieutenant Richard Milton.(6)

15th New York Independent Light Battery; Four 12-pdr. Napoleons. Capt. Patrick Hart.

Second Volunteer Brigade. Capt. Elijah D. Taft.
2nd Connecticut Artillery; Four 14-pdr. James Rifles, Two 12-pdr. Howitzers. Capt. John W. Sterling.

5th New York Independent Battery. Three 20-pdr. Parrott Rifles. Capt. Elijah Taft.(6)

Third Volunteer Brigade. Capt. James Huntington.

1st New Hampshire Light, Battery A. Six 3-inch Ordnance Rifles. Capt. Frederic M. Edgell.

1st Ohio Light Artillery, Battery H. Six 3- inch Ordnance Rifles. Lt. George W. Norton.

1st Pennsylvania Light Battery, F & G; Two 3-inch Ordnance Rifles. Capt. Bruce Ricketts.(6)

1st West Virginia Light, Battery C. Four 10-pdr. Parrott Rifles. Capt. Wallace Hill.

Fourth Volunteer Brigade. Capt. Robert H. Fitzhugh.

6th Maine Light, Battery F. Four 12-pdr. Napoleons. Lt. Edwin B. Dow.

1st New Jersey Light, Battery A. Six 3-inch Ordnance Rifles. Lt. Augustin N. Parsons.

1st New York Light, Battery G. Six 12-pdr. Napoleons. Capt. Nelson Ames.

1st New York, Battery K. Four 3-inch Ordnance Rifles. Capt. Robert Fitzhugh.

11th New York Independent Battery. Two 3-inch Ordnance Rifles. Capt. John E. Burton (Attached to 1st New York Battery K).

First Horse Artillery Reserve Brigade. Capt. James Robertson.

9th Michigan Light, Battery I. Six 3-inch Ordnance Rifles. Capt. Jabez J. Daniels.

Unattached

3rd Pennsylvania Heavy Artillery, Battery H. Two 3-inch Ordnance Rifles. Capt. William Rank.

10th New York Independent Battery. Temporarily broken up. Men assigned to Phillip's 5th Massachusetts and Taft's 5th New York.

14th New York Independent Battery. Temporarily broken up. Men assigned to Rogers' 1st New York battery B and Hart's 15th New York.

12-Pounder Napoleon

The bronze Napoleon was designed to fire spherical solid shot, case shot, shell and canister, with relative safety to the men manning the piece. The 4.62-inch smoothbore cannon was invented by Napoleon III in Europe in the early 1850s as a close-combat fieldgun. Adapted by the Federal Army in 1857, it was updated and quickly became the workhorse of the light artillery. Capable of sending a solid 12-pound iron ball 1,700 yards with a 2.5-pound powder charge, it became the chosen weapon used against massed infantry. A proven weapon at close quarters, its canister fire was deadly. The canister cylinder of the 12-pounder had twenty seven 1.5-inch balls that when fired scattered like a giant shotgun and were extremely lethal at 400 yards or less, the large bore allowed the balls to spread out almost as soon as the rounds left the muzzle.

3-Inch Ordnance Rifle

The iron 3-inch Ordnance Rifle was the superior light weapon with rifled bore. The spiral grooves running the length of the bore forced a projectile, when fired, to spin, allowing for greater velocity and distance, and also greater accuracy. The small 3.0-inch bore dampened the rifles' use as a close combat cannon as the small cylinder of canister was not large enough to inflict as much damage as that of the 12-pounder Napoleon. Well adapted for long range, it sent a 3-inch shell 1,850 yards (maximum killing range) with a small 1.0-pound powder charge, at 5 degrees elevation. Used for counter-battery fire, it inflicted considerable damage to batteries that the smoothbored guns could not otherwise reach. The preferred shell used against Pickett's attacking columns was the 3-inch timed case Schenkl shell, often called shrapnel.

10 & 20-Pounder Parrott Rifle

The Parrott rifle appeared at Gettysburg in its the 2.9-inch 10-pounder and 3.67-inch 20-pounder forms. All the Federal Parrott Rifles were made at the West Point Foundry located in Cold Springs, New York. Named after Robert Parker Parrott, formerly a U.S.army ordnance officer, it was not used as extensively as the three-inch Ordnance Rifle. With a one-pound charge the 10 pounder could hurtle a shell at five degrees elevation 2,000 yards. It had a range superior to that of the Ordnance Rifle but was far inferior in accuracy. A special solid bolt was designed to be used by the Parrott, but shell was usually preferred. Three of the 3.67-inch rifled cannons fired 20-pound case shells into the Confederates left flank during Pickett's Charge with devastating effect.

Profectiles Used During Pickett's Charge
Solid Shot

Made from molded cast iron, the solid projectile (round fixed for smoothbores, and conical for rifled cannon) was principally used for long-range fire against massed infantry, fortified positions and structures and in counter-battery fire. It was very useful against infantry posted under cover in woods and orchards. Smoothbore batteries fired solid shot during Pickett's initial appearance and beginning advance from Seminary Ridge to the Emmitsburg Road, as well as when Pickett's men retreated.

Case Shot ("Shrapnel")

A thin-walled iron projectile filled with musket balls in molten sulfur or rosin. Spherical case was used in the smoothbores while the rifled cannons fired a cone-shaped shell. Case shot contained a powder charge in the core which was ignited by a carefully cut timed fuse that itself was ignited on the cannon's firing. With the proper powder charge in the cannon, the shell would fly the determined distance and explode before impact, covering a large area with deadly missiles and small fragments. Principally used against attacking infantry, closing from maximum range to within 450 yards.

Shell

A thick-walled hollow iron projectile filled with black powder. Used against infantry and in counter-battery fire. The spherical shell was detonated by a fuse that was set in either a wooden or metallic fuse plug. They used two types of fuses: timed or percussion. The firing of the gun ignited the timed fuse. The conical timed-fuse shells were supposed to explode in the same manner as the spherical shell, but tended to bury themselves nose first into the ground prior to detonation, thus minimizing their killing power. The percussion shell was detonated on impact by a zinc plunger (cap) which struck and sparked a musket nipple attached to a "slider" onto a "anvil." The explosion that followed filled the immediate area with large fragments that tore flesh into shreds.

Canister

A thin-walled tin can filled with iron balls packed in sawdust, used at close quarters on attacking infantry with a killing range of 400 yards or less. At extreme close combat, double and triple loads could be fired. A good smoothbore artillery crew could ram home and fire up to three or four charges per minute. Canister was the real killer, causing extensive damage to Pickett's right flank regiments as they moved north toward the Copse of Trees.

Acknowledgements

Many individuals have given their encouragement and assistance in this project. I would like to thank Colonel Jacob Sheads and Dr. Bill Ridinger for getting me started and Elwood Christ, Charles Hathaway, John Jackson, Wayne Motts, George Otott, John Peterson and Harry Thaete for their help. The staffs of the Huntington Library, Los Angeles Public Library, United States Military History Institute at the Carlisle Barracks and the Drum Barracks Civil War Museum helped gather sources.

Kelly Stewart's editing skills are much in evidence. Good friends and family made life easier than it might have been. I want to thank especially Cliff, Peggy, Julie and Ermine Bream; my mother and father, Aunt Rosie, Greg King, Brian Ipjian, Jesse Ogden, Mable Pierce, Jim and Lori Shultz, Shannon and Dave Marzalek, and Sammy, Dillon, Darren and Dustin. Without the daily support, inspiration, understanding and love of Winona, I could not have even begun to think about undertaking this work.

David Shultz grew up in Harrisburg, Pennsylvania, and spent a good portion of his youth walking the Gettysburg battlefield. He developed an appreciation for artillery while serving in that branch. He lives in Southern California and is a member of the Civil War Round Table of Long Beach. He is currently working on an in-depth study of Federal artillery at Gettysburg.